T0328399

Corporate Social Responsibility

For Heather,
Kennedy, Marin & Stuart

Corporate Social Responsibility

Definition, Core Issues, and Recent Developments

Brent D. Beal

The University of Texas at Tyler

Los Angeles | London | New Delhi
Singapore | Washington DC

Los Angeles | London | New Delhi
Singapore | Washington DC

FOR INFORMATION:

SAGE Publications, Inc.

2455 Teller Road

Thousand Oaks, California 91320

E-mail: order@sagepub.com

SAGE Publications Ltd.

1 Oliver's Yard

55 City Road

London, EC1Y 1SP

United Kingdom

SAGE Publications India Pvt. Ltd.

B 1/I 1 Mohan Cooperative Industrial Area

Mathura Road, New Delhi 110 044

India

SAGE Publications Asia-Pacific Pte. Ltd.

3 Church Street

#10–04 Samsung Hub

Singapore 049483

Acquisitions Editor: Patricia Quinlin

Editorial Assistant: Katie Guarino

Production Editor: Stephanie Palermini

Typesetter: Hurix Systems Pvt. Ltd.

Proofreader: Laura Webb

Cover Designer: Anupama Krishnan

Marketing Manager: Liz Thornton

Permissions Editor: Jennifer Barron

Copyright © 2014 by SAGE Publications, Inc.

Printed in the United States of America

Library of Congress Cataloging-in-Publication Data

Beal, Brent D.
Corporate social responsibility: definition, core issues, and recent developments / Brent D. Beal, The University of Texas at Tyler.

pages cm
Includes bibliographical references and index.

ISBN 978-1-4522-9156-7 (pbk. : alk. paper) — ISBN 978-1-4833-1353-5 (web pdf) 1. Social responsibility of business. I. Title.

HD60.B42 2014
658.4′08—dc23   2013019403

This book is printed on acid-free paper.

13 14 15 16 17 10 9 8 7 6 5 4 3 2 1

Contents

Preface

I'm a professor of management in a college of business. In management textbooks, at least, the tenet of maximizing shareholder wealth is alive and well. It is often presented as the raison d'etre of the modern corporation.

Although maximizing shareholder wealth may be an important business objective, it is essential that we not confuse means for ends. Although maximizing shareholder may be, in many situations, the most effective means of contributing to the good of society, it should not be viewed as an end in itself. We—as in, society—expect our economic system to deliver certain outcomes, and we expect participants in that economic system—individuals and companies—to know what those outcomes are and to contribute to their realization. That is the essence of corporate social responsibility (CSR).

The difference between means and ends becomes painfully obvious, of course, when it becomes clear that market participants have pursued profit in ways that have harmed the rest of us. If an industry generates a hundred million dollars in profits, for example, but imposes a billion dollars of costs on third parties, pretty profit and loss statements usually aren't enough to stop folks from going home and getting their torches and pitchforks.

The reason business students have a hard time seeing this is because they aren't used to conceptualizing business activity—and economic markets—as parts of a larger social system. They aren't used to thinking in terms of embeddedness, mutual interdependence, social control, and value creation (rather than profit maximization).

Once it is understood that the primary purpose of our economic system is to deliver the macroeconomic outcomes that society expects of it, and that participants in that system have an obligation—a social obligation—to contribute to those outcomes, everything else falls into place. When should companies focus on maximizing shareholder wealth? Answer: When doing so results in the creation of economic value, and thereby contributes to the social good. When should companies allow other factors besides shareholder wealth to influence their decisions? Answer: When maximizing shareholder wealth won't lead to the creation of economic value, and therefore won't contribute to the social good. A critical part of CSR is knowing the difference. In theory, at least, it really is that simple.

In practice, things are more complicated. This book is a product of an ongoing conversation I've had with my students over the last ten years. It represents a perspective that I believe is missing from most business textbooks. CSR has become an important part of doing business in the twenty-first century. For that reason alone, business students need to be exposed to it. As I argue in the book, however, there is more at stake than just being prepared for the job market. CSR has the potential, if properly implemented, to make economic markets more transparent, efficient, and effective in serving societal interests. And that's something we should all care about.

I owe a debt to my students. Hopefully they've benefitted from the running conversation I've obligated them to be a part of over the years.

I thank Heather Olson Beal for encouragement and editing. I thank Cristina Neesham for the running conversation we've had about many of the ideas in this book. I thank administrators, colleagues, and staff who have helped me along the way. I thank The University of Texas at Tyler for giving me an academic home during process. I thank Patricia Quinlin, Katie Guarino, and others at SAGE for their contributions to the project.

Finally, I thank the following reviewers for their conscientious input: William Acar (PhD), Kent State University; Daniel C. Bochsler, Naveen Jindal School of Management, University of Texas at Dallas; Amod Choudhary, City University of New York, Lehman College; Robert D. Gulbro, Athens State University; W. M. Hayden Jr., PhD, P.E., CMQ/OE, University at Buffalo, School of Management; E. Nicole Hess-Escalante, The University of Texas at San Antonio;

Dr. Jim Kerner, Athens State University, Athens, Alabama; R. Kernochan, California State University, Northridge; Jim Muraski, Marquette University; Stephanie E. Newell, Eastern Michigan University; Herb Nold, Polk State College; David Olson, California State University, Bakersfield; John A. Parnell, PhD, University of North Carolina—Pembroke; Brandon Randolph-Seng, Texas A&M University-Commerce; Veronica Rosas-Tatum, Palo Alto College; Stephen Takach, University of Texas at San Antonio; Zelimir William Todorovic, Indiana University-Purdue University Fort Wayne; Isaac Wanasika, Monfort College of Business, University of Northern Colorado.

Introduction

Corporate social responsibility (CSR) is part of the reality of doing business in the twenty-first century. Regardless of how one feels about it, CSR is here to stay. As one prominent critic expressed it, "the movement for corporate social responsibility has won the battle of ideas."[i] Most Fortune 500 companies now include a senior-level position in their organizational structure dedicated to CSR and/or sustainability issues. Reporting standards are beginning to solidify and diffuse. The Global Reporting Initiative, for example, a non-profit organization dedicated to promoting economic, environmental and social sustainability, produces a comprehensive sustainability reporting framework that is being rapidly adopted by organizations around the world, and third parties, like KPMG, are beginning to audit corporate responsibility reports and issue assurance statements.[ii] In 2009, Bloomberg added environmental, social, and governance (or ESG) indicators to its terminal data stream. [iii]

Business activity is inextricably linked to larger issues related to proper market functioning and the promotion of general societal welfare. From a CSR perspective, although firms may strive to maximize shareholder wealth, the purpose of the corporation is not to enrich its owners, but to contribute to the economic well-being of the social system of which it is a part. The genius of properly functioning economic markets is that often the most effective way of doing the latter (i.e., contributing to societal economic well-being) is by striving to do the former (i.e., maximize shareholder wealth). In other words, from a CSR perspective, profit maximization is a means to an end, rather than an end in itself.

CSR is important for both society and business. For example, as the most recent global financial crisis demonstrated, economic markets do not always produce optimal outcomes. In this case, as in other significant cases of corporate malfeasance and market failure, there was an immediate escalation of calls for increased regulatory oversight. To the degree that CSR is able to constrain and guide the behavior of market participants in ways that improve market outcomes, it has the potential to reduce the need for external regulation. Society benefits from improved economic outcomes and reduced regulatory obligations, and business benefits from increased trust and greater latitude for autonomous activity.

CSR is not about pressuring firms into engaging in philanthropy or obligating them to shoulder additional responsibility for different social problems. Considered broadly, CSR is about establishing and perpetuating social norms that make economic markets more transparent and effective in serving societal interests. As we move further into the twenty-first century, CSR is likely to become an increasingly essential framework for reconciling individual interests and the social good. Because of this, CSR is likely to play an increasingly influential role in every aspect of business, from corporate strategy to marketing and human resource management.

As the title suggests, the purpose of this book is to introduce CSR by defining it, identifying its most essential elements, and highlighting recent developments. The chapters are intended to build on each other, beginning with a broad definition of CSR in the first chapter and culminating in a discussion of new developments and different conceptual frames in the last chapter. There is some difficult—but critical—material in between, including sections on important CSR assumptions, the perfect competition market model, market failure, social dilemmas, value creation, and the business case for CSR.

Although the details are important, keep the big picture in mind. CSR, considered broadly, is about how our economic system should be structured and the responsibility of participants in it to contribute to outcomes that benefit us all.

ENDNOTES

[i]This comment prefaced an article on CSR that appeared in the *Economist* in 2005: Crook, C. 2005. The good company. *Economist*, 374(8410): Special Section, 3–4.

[ii]See these articles on the diffusion of sustainability reporting standards: Cecil, L. 2008. Corporate social responsibility reporting in the United States. *McNair Scholars Research Journal*, 1(1): Article 6; Fifka, M. S. and Drabble, M. 2012. Focus and standardization of sustainability reporting— A comparative study of the United Kingdom and Finland. *Business Strategy and the Environment*, 21(7): 455–474; Marimon, F., Alonso-Almeida, M. d. M., Rodríguez, M. d. P. and Cortez Alejandro, K. A. 2012. The worldwide diffusion of the global reporting initiative: What is the point? *Journal of Cleaner Production*, 33(2012): 132–144; Morhardt, J. E. 2010. Corporate social responsibility and sustainability reporting on the internet. *Business Strategy & the Environment*, 19(7): 436–452; Perego, P. and Kolk, A. 2012. Multinationals' accountability on sustainability: The evolution of third-party assurance of sustainability reports. *Journal of Business Ethics*, 110(2): 173–190; Pounder, B. 2011. Trends in sustainability reporting. *Strategic Finance*, 93(6): 21–23.

[iii]Tullis, P. 2011. Making the bottom line green. *Fast Company*, 154: 36–37.

1

What is CSR?

Although the role of business in society has been debated for hundreds of years, if not longer, the concept of corporate social responsibility (or CSR) in its current form first emerged in the 1950s.[i] A convenient marker for the start of the modern CSR era is the publication, in 1953, of Howard R. Bowen's book, *Social Responsibilities of the Businessman*.

The same questions that motivated Bowen remain relevant today. What responsibilities do businesses have to contribute in positive ways to society? What benefits might be derived from a more enthusiastic assumption of these responsibilities? What practical steps could be taken to encourage businesses to give greater weight to these responsibilities in their decision making?

Here's another way to think of CSR.

One of the defining characteristics of properly functioning economic markets is the alignment of individual and collective interests. If individual and collective interests are aligned, then there is no need for participants—either suppliers (i.e. companies) or buyers (often individuals)—to consider the impact of their actions on market outcomes. For example, in properly functioning economic markets, it is assumed that self-interested behavior by both buyers and sellers will produce desirable outcomes, such as efficient utilization and optimal allocation of resources. Adam Smith referred to this alignment as an "invisible hand" when he observed that individuals, focusing only on their own self-interest, and without giving any consideration to the broader impact of their actions, seem to behave as if guided by an unseen force to promote societal interests.

In other words, in properly functioning markets, participants can, in a sense, outsource their concern for societal interests to the invisible hand. Participants can simply shrug their shoulders, assume that the market will sort it out, and go about pursuing their own interests. Remarkably, as Adam Smith observed, by focusing on their own interests, market participants often end up promoting societal interests more effectively than if they had intentionally set out to do so.

In this respect, CSR runs counter to market logic. Because markets do not always function properly, there is no guarantee that the pursuit of individual interests will further societal interests. Businesses, therefore, are expected to actively assess the effect of their actions on the broader economic and social systems in which they are embedded. From a CSR perspective, therefore, businesses should be aware of societal expectations, and they should intentionally regulate their behavior in order to contribute to outcomes that meet those expectations.

Consider this. What if participants in the housing and mortgage markets prior to the global financial crisis of 2007–2008 had more carefully considered the potential impact of their actions on the broader economy? What if some of the key players had allowed these broader considerations to constrain their self-interested behavior? Might the crisis have been less severe, or have been avoided altogether?

The general idea of CSR, therefore, is that businesses have a responsibility to contribute to economic outcomes that meet societal expectations. Although this general statement is relatively uncontroversial, it is surprisingly difficult to provide a more precise definition.

DEFINITIONS

The CEO of ExxonMobil, Rex Tillerson, recently commented that "there is a wide diversity of views on the role of a company such as ExxonMobil in today's society. We know that we will never satisfy everyone."[ii]

In the sixty years since Bowen's landmark book, numerous definitions of CSR have been offered by academics, practitioners, councils, and groups. The five definitions included below are arranged in chronological order and illustrate a few of the different ways CSR has been conceptualized and defined. As you read these definitions, look for both commonalities and differences.

The term social responsibilities of businessmen will be used frequently. It refers to the obligations of businessmen [and businesswomen] to pursue those policies, to make those decisions, or to follow those lines of action which are desirable in terms of the objectives and values of our society. This definition does not imply that businessmen as members of society lack the rights to criticize the values. . . . It is assumed, however, that as servants of society, they must not disregard socially accepted values or place their own values above those of society.–Howard R. Bowen, 1953[iii]

All of this suggests that when we invoke the phrase "the social responsibilities of the businessman [or businesswoman]," we mean that businessmen [or businesswomen] should oversee the operation of an economic system that fulfills the expectations of the public. And this means in turn that the economy's means of production should be employed in such a way that production and distribution should enhance total socio-economic welfare. Social responsibility in the final analysis implies a public posture toward society's economic and human resources and a willingness to see that those resources are utilized for broad social ends and not simply for the narrowly circumscribed interests of private persons and firms.–William C. Frederick, 1960[iv]

What does it mean to say that the corporate executive has a "social responsibility" in his capacity as businessman? If this statement is not pure rhetoric, it must mean that he is to act in some way that is not in the interest of his employers. . . . That is why, in my book Capitalism and Freedom, *I have called it a "fundamentally subversive doctrine" in a free society, and have said that in such a society, "there is one and only one social responsibility of business—to use its resources and engage in activities designed to increase its profits so long as it stays within the rules of the game, which is to say, engages in open and free competition without deception or fraud.–Milton Friedman, 1970*[v]

With so many conflicting goals and objectives, the definition of CSR is not always clear. Here we define CSR as actions that appear to further some social good, beyond the interests of the firm and that which is required by law. This definition underscores that, to us, CSR means going beyond obeying the law.–Abagail McWilliams & Donald Siegel, 2001[vi]

Corporate social responsibility (CSR) is about how businesses align their values and behaviour with the expectations and needs of stakeholders—not just customers and investors, but also employees, suppliers, communities, regulators, special interest groups and society as a whole. CSR describes a company's commitment to be accountable to its stakeholders. CSR demands that businesses manage the economic, social and environmental impacts of their operations to maximise the benefits and minimise the downsides. Key CSR issues include governance, environmental management, stakeholder engagement, labour standards, employee and community relations, social equity, responsible sourcing and human rights.–Two Tomorrows, 2013[vii]

Although these definitions contain similar elements, it should also be clear that there is significant disagreement. It is important to realize that defining CSR is not merely a descriptive exercise. It is not as simple as attaching a label to a particular business practice, as is the case with many other business concepts. It is a normative exercise in the sense that defining CSR requires making the role of business in society explicit by enumerating societal obligations. Taken far enough, defining CSR becomes a political or ideological exercise, because it requires the implementation of a vision of how society's political economy should be structured, bounded, and ultimately, controlled.[viii] It shouldn't be surprising that there is little agreement on the specifics. CSR is, by its nature, an "essentially contested concept."[ix]

Despite these challenges, this book builds on previous definitions by proposing the following definition of CSR:

CSR, broadly defined, is the moral and practical obligation of market participants to consider the effect of their actions on collective or system-level outcomes and to then regulate their behavior in order to contribute to bringing those outcomes into congruence with societal expectations.[x]

Milton Friedman, an economist and recipient of the Nobel Prize in Economic Sciences, is generally perceived to have been hostile to the CSR concept. Did it surprise you to find a quote from him included with the other CSR definitions? Go back and reread the paragraph attributed to him. Note that while criticizing the concept of CSR as he perceives it, he provides his own definition of it: "There is one and only one social responsibility of business—to use its resources and engage in activities designed to increase its profits so long as it stays within the rules of the game, which is to say, engages in open and free competition without deception or fraud." From Friedman's perspective, the best way for individual companies to contribute to societal welfare is to maximize profits (subject to certain constraints). Friedman's comments are included with other definitions of CSR because he explicitly links the behavior of individual businesses to societal welfare, albeit in a different way than most CSR advocates. We will discuss Friedman's position in greater detail in Chapter 3.

REPORTING & MEASUREMENT

Up to this point, CSR has been discussed in relatively abstract terms. A reasonable question to ask, therefore, is what does CSR looks like in practice? What do businesses do that qualifies as CSR?

An early textbook on business society, originally published in 1966, listed the following areas of potential social involvement: ecology and environmental quality (e.g., pollution, aesthetics, noise control), consumerism (e.g., product safety), community needs (e.g., urban renewal), business giving, minorities and disadvantaged persons (e.g., training, utilization in supply chain), and labor relations, among others.[xi]

Third parties, like the Global Reporting Initiative (GRI), have developed and promoted different reporting guidelines that involve hundreds of different indicators and data points.[xii] The G3.1 framework, the latest version of GRI's reporting guidelines, for example, involves detailed indicators across three principle areas: economic, environmental, and social. In the social area, GRI guidelines identify four subcategories: labor practices, human rights, society, and product responsibility. Specific performance indicators in the social subcategory include the percentage of operations with local engagement programs, the percentage of business units analyzed for risks related to corruption, and the total number of legal actions for anti-competitive behavior, anti-trust, and monopoly practices, among others.[xiii] AccountAbility, another third-party organization promoting sustainability reporting, has developed the AA1000 framework that involves a similarly comprehensive set of indicators.

CSR information was recently added to Bloomberg terminals—a proprietary computer system marketed by Bloomberg L. P. and used by financial service professionals that streams real-time financial data and provides access to the company's electronic trading platform. Referred to as environmental, social, and governance data (or ESG data), Bloomberg publishes more than two hundred indicators, including the number of board meetings per year, the size of the audit committee, total employee fatalities, whether or not the company is a UN Global Compact signatory, municipal water use, and other similar variables.

Researchers have attempted to measure CSR by relying primarily on three types of information: a) reputational scores or rankings, generally based on survey responses (e.g., *Fortune* magazine's Corporate Reputation Survey[xiv]) b) third-party composite measures, indices or rankings (e.g., the KLD's social performance ratings[xv]), and c) analysis of company documents, filings, observation of activities or other direct data-gathering efforts (e.g., content analysis of annual company reports, media reports, or interviews with company representatives). Measures of CSR have included, among other things, pollution performance ratings, concern for the disadvantaged, the effectiveness of employee training programs, the existence of sexual harassment policies, and workplace safety records. Because CSR is often defined so broadly, research studies have employed a wide range of different—and in many ways, incompatible—empirical measures. [xvi]

Table 1.1 includes links to the websites of the top ten companies on the 2012 Best Corporate Citizens list published by *CR Magazine*.[xvii] To get a better understanding of what CSR looks like in practice, spend a few minutes reviewing the information these companies disclose about their CSR activities. For example, as of June 1, 2013, Bristol-Myers Squibb provided an update on its ten-year sustainability goals (established in 2001), outlined its 2015 goals, and provided access to a comprehensive sustainability report, audited by a third party, that adhered to the 2006 G3 reporting guidelines developed by GRI.

Specific examples of other CSR activities, again, as of June 1, 2013, included IBM's energy conservation projects (that resulted in savings equivalent to 7.4% of the firm's total energy use in 2011), Intel's employee volunteer program (that involved 1.1 million hours of service at 5,100 schools and nonprofits in 45 countries in 2011), Microsoft's work with the British Council to help ministries of education and other stakeholders equip schools in Ghana, Nigeria,

TABLE 1.1   Top Ten Companies on *CR Magazine's* 2012 List of the 100 Best Corporate Citizens

	Company	Symbol	Company Website
1	Bristol-Myers Squibb Co.	BMY	http://www.bms.com
2	International Business Machines Corp.	IBM	http://www.ibm.com
3	Intel Corp.	INTC	http://www.intel.com
4	Microsoft Corporation	MSFT	http://www.microsoft.com
5	Johnson Controls Inc	JCI	http://www.johnsoncontrols.com
6	Accenture PLC	ACN	http://www.accenture.com
7	Spectra Energy Corp.	SE	http://www.spectraenergy.com
8	Campbell Soup Co.	CPB	http://www.campbellsoupcompany.com
9	Nike, Inc.	NKE	http://www.nikeinc.com
10	Freeport-McMoRan Copper & Gold Inc.	FCX	http://www.fcx.com

Source: Corporate Responsibility Magazine. http://www.thecro.com/

Uganda, Ethiopia, Kenya, and Tanzania with server hubs to be used in training local teachers and students, and Johnson Control's ongoing commitment to operating in accordance with the ten principles of the UN Global Compact. More detailed information about these initiatives—and hundreds of other CSR programs and initiatives—are available on the websites of the ten companies in Table 1.1.

Similar information is now available from the majority of large companies. According to a recent report by KPMG, for example, 95% of the largest global companies now regularly report on corporate responsibility activities.[xviii] The scope of activities and level of detail reflected in these reports offers an unprecedented look at aspects of corporate activity that are often only indirectly represented in traditional financial statements.

Over the last ten years, the amount of CSR and sustainability data published annually by the world's largest corporations has increased exponentially. Comprehensive reporting frameworks are beginning to emerge and there is a growing consensus regarding reporting protocols and standards. This trend attests to the significant progress that continues to be made in the area of CSR disclosure and assessment.

MAPPING THE TERRAIN

The objective of financial accounting is to provide information about the economic performance of businesses. The objective of corporate responsibility reporting is to provide additional information about aspects of business performance that may not be fully reflected in financial data. It is important to recognize that corporate responsibility reporting is intended to supplement financial accounting data, not replace it.

In a philosophical sense, it is relatively easy to assert that a society's economic system is designed to yield certain outcomes, and that businesses should therefore incorporate these outcomes into their decision making. In practice, however, the question of exactly what actions constitute CSR is complex. The 2012 Best Corporate Citizens list referenced earlier, for example, was compiled based on an analysis of 318 individual variables across seven major activity categories and fourteen related subcategories. Each of these variables was collected for each company considered for inclusion on the list.

In an effort to represent the relationship between business and society in a conceptually simple way, a number of different CSR models have been proposed.

Concentric Circle Model

The Committee for Economic Development published a statement in 1971 suggesting that societal expectations could be represented by three concentric circles of responsibilities (see Figure 1.1).[xix] The inner circle includes traditional economic responsibilities directly related to the efficiency of business functions. The next circle out—the intermediate circle—represents the responsibility to carry out the activities of the first circle in a manner consistent with evolving societal values and shifting priorities. If, for example, society elevates its expectations regarding environmental stewardship, or employee safety, then businesses would have a responsibility to incorporate these changes into their decision-making processes. Finally, the outer circle represents emergent or ambiguous expectations, often associated with complex social

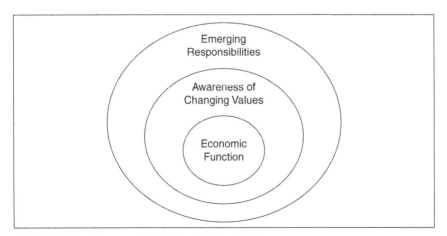

FIGURE 1.1   Concentric Circle Model of CSR

Source: Adapted from Committee for Economic Development. 1971. *Social Responsibilities for Business Corporations.* New York: Author; and Blomstrom, R. L. 1971. *Business, Society, and Environment: Social Power and Social Response* (2nd ed.), New York: McGraw-Hill Book Company.

problems, such as income inequality or poverty. In terms of priority, businesses are expected to begin with the inner circle and work their way outward.

The CSR Pyramid

In 1991, Archie B. Carroll argued in an academic paper that CSR could be subdivided into four primary components and that these components could be visualized as a pyramid (see Figure 1.2).[xx] At the base of the pyramid are economic responsibilities. At their core, businesses are economic entities designed to be driven by the potential for profit. Other responsibilities are dependent on a business first fulfilling its economic responsibilities, because unless it is able to do so, it will be unable to continue in operation. Legal responsibilities are represented by the next layer of the pyramid. Although businesses are expected to pursue economic profit, they are expected to do so within the framework of laws and regulations established by society. The third layer is comprised of ethical responsibilities. Although laws and regulations are rooted in ethical norms and the ideals of fairness of justice, there is a significant subset of societal standards, norms, and expectations that have not been codified into law, but with which businesses should nevertheless comply. Businesses should recognize that there is constant interplay between the legal and ethical layers as societal expectations evolve and laws are changed. Finally, the last layer represents philanthropic responsibilities. This layer includes efforts intended to promote the general welfare in ways that may be appreciated, but are not necessarily expected.

Based on the pyramid model of CSR, businesses should start at the base—beginning with economic responsibilities—and then work to satisfy legal and ethical responsibilities before finally reaching the top, where they can address philanthropic responsibilities.

Although both of these CSR models are conceptually appealing in some ways, they both imply that the economic function of business can be separated from other less central (and therefore, less important) considerations. In the case of the Concentric Model of CSR, for example, it is implied that the economic function of businesses should be given priority over an awareness of shifting

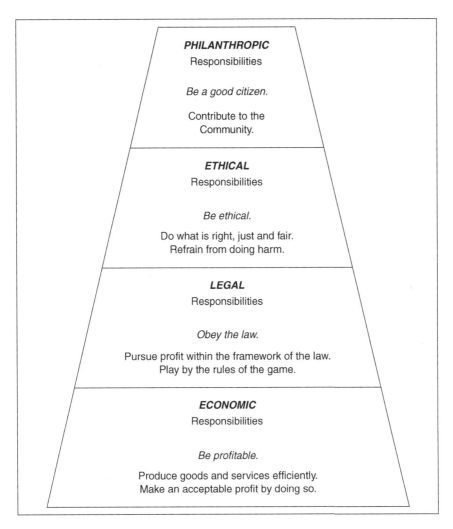

FIGURE 1.2 The CSR Pyramid

Source: Adapted from Carroll, A. B. 1991. The pyramid of coporate social responsibility: Toward the moral management of organizational stakeholders. *Business Horizons*, 34:39–48.

societal values and priorities. Shifting values and priorities, however, are reflected in both supplier and buyer value attributions, and are therefore directly related to the prices the company is asked to pay by suppliers and the prices customers are willing to pay for the company's products and services. In other words, an awareness of shifting values and priorities isn't something a business should consider after it addresses its economic function; this awareness is an essential part *of* its economic function.

Similarly, in the case of the CSR Pyramid, CSR requires firms to pursue their economic interests *subject to* legal and ethical considerations, not the other way around. In other words, legal and ethical considerations should constrain and shape the pursuit of economic interests rather than be treated as secondary objectives to be pursued after economic responsibilities have been addressed.

Despite these shortcomings, both of these models have been influential in shaping how CSR has been conceptualized.

RELATED TERMS

CSR should not be thought of as a single idea or concept, but rather as an "umbrella" term that unites a number of different approaches or perspectives that explicitly address the relationship between business and society from a business perspective. For this reason, some academics have suggested that CSR should be conceptualized as a field of study, rather than a specific term with an agreed-upon meaning.[xxi] It shouldn't be surprising that there are a number of associated concepts and terms that need to be briefly mentioned.

Sustainability, and the more specific term, corporate sustainability, are both rooted historically in efforts by the United Nations to promote sustainable development, defined as "development that meets the needs of the present without compromising the ability of future generations to meet their own needs."[xxii] Although in the past it has been associated primarily with environmental stewardship, it is now understood that sustainability, when used in a business context, encompasses economic and social concerns, as well as environmental issues. Evolving CSR reporting standards, such as GRI's reporting framework, have largely adopted this same structure (i.e., a tripartite focus on economic, social, and environmental responsibilities). In its current form, the term sustainability is more or less synonymous with CSR, and in certain contexts (e.g., in academic circles in Europe), it now appears to be the preferred label for efforts to address the business and society interface.

Corporate citizenship is another concept that is often associated with CSR. Corporate citizenship tends to be more practitioner-based than CSR, and is centered around the idea or metaphor of the corporation as a good neighbor or virtuous citizen.[xxiii] *Corporate social performance,* another related concept, adopts as a conceptual starting point the responsibility of businesses to sense and then respond to evolving social expectations.[xxiv] In the 1950s, CSR generally took the form of charitable giving; this history continues to be reflected in CSR's close association with *corporate philanthropy* and other forms of community involvement.[xxv]

At least two other related concepts deserve mention: *stakeholder theory* and *systems theory.* Stakeholder theory emerged in the early 1980s as a new way of thinking about corporate strategy.[xxvi] From a stakeholder perspective, instead of working primarily to maximize returns to shareholders, managers should consider the needs of a broad range of stakeholders, defined as "those groups and individuals that can affect, or are affected by, the accomplishment of organizational purpose."[xxvii] Managers should seek to guide the business in a way that creates value for all stakeholders. Some proponents of stakeholder theory have argued that CSR has outlived its usefulness and that it should be replaced by a focus on stakeholder responsibility or stakeholder management.[xxviii]

Systems theory, another term that is often associated with CSR, is a broad, interdisciplinary approach that focuses on the general characteristics of different systems, rather than specific fields of research. When applied to CSR, systems theory focuses on the embeddedness of businesses in their surrounding systems and subsystems, and draws attention to feedback loops, interdependencies, unintended consequences, and other system characteristics that are often essential to an understanding of the complex role of business in society. For example, system dynamics, a systems theory approach pioneered in the 1950s by Jay Forrester, focuses primarily on feedback loops, stocks and flows to explain why simple systems can often produce complex and nonlinear outcomes.

One example of the systemic nature of CSR is the issue of employee wages. Should companies, for example, be allowed to pay employees less than a subsistence or "living" wage?[xxix] If companies are allowed to do so, then should these employees be allowed to access social safety net programs?[xxx] If employees are paid less than a subsistence wage, but are willing (and able) to continue working because their wages are effectively subsidized by taxpayers, what implications does this have for the labor market? If competition among companies pushes down wages, and falling wages increase demand for social safety net programs, what implications does this have for the labor market? What implications does this have for tax policy?

Sustainability, corporate citizenship, corporate social performance, philanthropy, community involvement, stakeholder theory, and systems theory all represent important parts of what might be termed the CSR "ecosystem." Each of these related terms represents a different way of approaching the same overarching questions articulated by Bowen in 1953 and highlighted at the start of the chapter.

CHAPTER SUMMARY

A convenient marker for the start of the modern CSR era is the publication of the book *Social Responsibilities of the Businessman.* Published in 1953, this book asked "What responsibilities do businesses have to contribute in positive ways to society?" In many ways, CSR is an attempt to answer this question. This chapter offers a number of different definitions of CSR. For present purposes, CSR can be broadly defined as the moral and practical obligation of market participants to consider the effect of their actions on collective or system-level outcomes and to then regulate their behavior in order to contribute to bringing those outcomes into congruence with societal expectations.

A number of different organizations, such as the Global Reporting Initiative (GRI), have developed reporting guidelines that specify what types of CSR information businesses should report, and in what form they should report it. Nearly all of the largest global companies now regularly release corporate responsibility reports.

At least two well-known CSR models represent the broad relationship between business and society in a conceptually simple way: the Concentric Circle model and the CSR Pyramid. Although both of these models inappropriately compartmentalize economic, legal, and ethical considerations, both have been influential in shaping how CSR has been conceptualized.

A number of different terms are associated with CSR. Sustainability, corporate citizenship, corporate social performance, philanthropy, community involvement, stakeholder theory, and systems theory all represent important parts of what might be termed the CSR "ecosystem."

REVIEW QUESTIONS

1. A convenient marker for the start of the modern CSR era is the publication of Bowen's book, *Social Responsibilities of the Businessman*. What questions did Bowen ask in this book? Why are these questions still relevant today?

2. How is CSR different from Adam Smith's concept of the invisible hand? Why is this important?

3. Based on the definitions of CSR in the chapter—including the author's definition—what do you believe are the essential elements of CSR? Why?

4. Describe some of the CSR programs or activities you discovered on the websites of the companies listed in Table 1.1.

5. Briefly describe the Concentric Circle Model of CSR and the CSR Pyramid. Explain how these models inappropriately compartmentalize economic, legal, and ethical considerations.

6. List and briefly describe the CSR-related terms highlighted in the text: sustainability, corporate citizenship, corporate social performance, philanthropy, stakeholder theory, and systems theory.

APPENDIX: ADDITIONAL CSR DEFINITIONS

Here are some additional definitions of CSR (listed in chronological order):

The concept of social responsibilities is rather difficult to set forth, for there are many definitions. Briefly, however, the concept implies that the modern business corporation should recognize that, in this day and age, it can no longer hungrily pursue the single goal of profits to the complete neglect of its table manners. The idea of social responsibilities supposes that the corporation has not only economic and legal obligations, but also certain responsibilities to society which extend beyond these obligations. The corporation today must take an interest in politics, in the welfare of the community, in education, in the "happiness" of its employees—in fact, in the whole social world about it. In a sense, therefore, it must act "justly" as a proper citizen should.–Joseph W. McGuire, 1963[xxxi]

The difference between social responsibility and traditional business decision making is that traditional decision makers confine themselves primarily to narrow economic and technical values, but social responsibility extends thinking to social values as well. It also requires thinking in terms of the whole social system, rather than the narrow interests of a single organization, group, or person. It is clearly a systems way of thinking.–Keith Davis & Robert L. Blomstrom, 1966[xxxii]

The basic idea of corporate social responsibility is that business and society are interwoven rather than distinct entities; therefore, society has certain expectations for appropriate business behavior and outcomes.–Donna J. Wood, 1991[xxxiii]

Business needs a stable social environment that provides a predictable climate for investment and trade. CSR is the means by which business contributes to that stability rather than detracting from it. By establishing and maintaining a corporate agenda which recognizes social priorities and is tailored to meet them, business displays its human face to consumers, communities and opinion leaders.–World Business Council for Sustainable Development, 2000[xxxiv]

As the power and influence of businesses have grown, so have society's expectations. Not only does society now want corporations to take much more responsibility for their social and environmental impacts, but we now expect corporations to provide leadership and address pressing social challenges—narrow the gap between the rich and poor, solve poverty, reduce human-rights abuses. Corporate citizenship is now defined by what a company "does," not what it "gives."–Council on Foundations, 2012[xxxv]

Corporate social responsibility (CSR, also called corporate conscience, corporate citizenship, social performance, or sustainable responsible business) is a form of corporate self-regulation integrated into a business model. CSR policy functions as a built-in, self-regulating mechanism whereby a business monitors and ensures its active compliance with the spirit of the law, ethical standards, and international norms. CSR is a process with the aim to embrace responsibility for the company's actions and encourage a positive impact through its activities on the environment, consumers, employees, communities, stakeholders and all other members of the public sphere who may also be considered as stakeholders.—Wikipedia, 2013[xxxvi]

ENDNOTES

[i] For a more complete history of the CSR construct, see Carroll, A. B. 1999. Corporate social responsibility: Evolution of a definitional construct. *Business and Society,* 38(3): 268–296; also see Carroll, A. B. 2008. A history of corporate social responsibility: Concepts and practices. In A. Crane, A. McWilliams, D. Matten, J. Moon, and D. Siegel (Eds.), *The Oxford handbook of corporate social responsibility:* 19–46. Oxford: Oxford University Press.

[ii] This statement was made by Rex W. Tillerson, Chairman and CEO, in a recent letter to stakeholders. As of April 6, 2011, this letter was available on the company website: http://www.exxonmobil.com/Corporate/community_ccr_ceo.aspx.

[iii] Bowen, H. R. 1953. *Social responsibilities of the businessman.* New York: Harper & Row, see page 6.

[iv] Frederick, W. C. 1960. The growing concern over business responsibility. *California Management Review,* 2: 54–61, see page 60.

[v] Friedman, M. 1970. The social responsibility of business is to increase its profits. *New York Times Magazine,* September 13.

[vi] McWilliams, A. and Siegel, D. 2001. Corporate social responsibility: A theory of the firm perspective. *Academy of Management Review,* 26(1): 117–127, see page 117.

[vii] http://www.twotomorrows.com/news/what-csr/, accessed on Feb. 6, 2013.

[viii] For a good overview of the academic field of CSR scholarship, see Crane, A., McWilliams, A., Matten, D., Moon, J., and Siegel, D. 2008. The corporate social responsibility agenda. In A. Crane, A. McWilliams, D. Matten, J. Moon, and D. Siegel (Eds.), *The Oxford handbook of corporate social responsibility:* 3–15. Oxford: Oxford University Press. For more information on an interesting perspective on the ongoing discussion of CSR in academia that addresses the role of ideology, see Marens, R. 2004. Wobbling on a one-legged stool: The decline of American pluralism and the academic treatment of corporate social responsibility. *Journal of Academic Ethics,* 2(1): 63–87.

[ix] This phrase has been used to describe the concept of corporate citizenship, see Moon, J., Crane, A., and Matten, D. 2005. Can corporations be citizens? Corporate citizenship as a metaphor for business participation in society. *Business*

Ethics Quarterly, 15(3): 429–453. It is also been used to described the CSR construct: Crane, A., McWilliams, A., Matten, D., Moon, J., and Siegel, D. 2008. The corporate social responsibility agenda. In A. Crane, A. McWilliams, D. Matten, J. Moon, and D. Siegel (Eds.), *The Oxford handbook of corporate social responsibility:* 3–15. Oxford: Oxford University Press.

[x]This definition is adapted from a working paper on the systemic aspects of CSR by the author and a colleague: Beal, B. D. and Neesham, C. 2013. Systemic CSR: Insourcing the invisible hand. Tyler, TX: The University of Tyler at Texas.

[xi]Davis, K. and Blomstrom, R. L. 1975. *Business and society: Environment and responsibility* (3rd ed.). New York: McGraw-Hill, pgs. 8–10.

[xii]Detailed information on GRI's most recent update of its sustainability reporting framework (G3.1) is available on its website: https://www.globalreporting.org/Pages/default.aspx.

[xiii]For a good overview of different CSR and sustainability reporting standards, see Marimon, F., Alonso-Almeida, M. d. M., Rodríguez, M. d. P., and Cortez Alejandro, K. A. 2012. The worldwide diffusion of the global reporting initiative: What is the point? *Journal of Cleaner Production,* 33(2012): 132–144.

[xiv]The utility of the Fortune index for CSR research remains a subject of debate: Fryxell, G. E. and Jia, W. 1994. The Fortune corporate 'reputation' index: Reputation for what? *Journal of Management,* 20(1): 1; Brown, B. and Perry, S. 1994. Removing the financial performance halo from fortune's "most admired" companies. *Academy of Management Journal,* 37(5): 1347–1359; Brown, B. and Perry, S. 1995. Halo-removed residuals of *Fortune's* "responsibility to the community and environment": A decade of data. *Business & Society,* 34: 199–215; Wood, D. J. and Jones, R. E. 1995. Stakeholder mismatching: A theoretical problem in empirical research on corporate social performance. *International Journal of Organizational Analysis (1993—2002),* 3(3): 229.

[xv]Kinder, Lydenberg, Domini & Co. (KLD) was founded in 1989. The company produced a social performance rating, or KLD rating, for a number of publicly traded firms. KLD is credited with creating the first social investment benchmark, the Domini 4000 SocialSM Index or DS 400 Index (a socially screened, capitalization-weighted index of 400 common stocks). KLD was acquired by RiskMetrics Group in 2009. RiskMetrics was then acquired by MSCI Inc. in 2010. More information on MSCI can be found here: http://www.msci.com/about/. The DS 400 Index is now referred to as the MSCI KLD 400 Social Index.

[xvi]For a good discussion of some of the challenges of measuring CSR in empirical academic studies, see Aupperle, K. E., Carroll, A. B., and Hatfield, J. D. 1985. An empirical examination of the relationship between corporate social responsibility and profitability. *Academy of Management Journal,* 28(2): 446–463; Also see Abbott, W. F. and Monsen, R. J. 1979. On the measurement of corporate social responsibility: Self-reported disclosures as a method of measuring corporate social involvement. *Academy of Management Journal,* 22(3): 501–515, and Wood, D. J. 2010. Measuring corporate social performance: A review. *International Journal of Management Reviews,* 12(1): 50–84.

[xvii]*CR Magazine* (or *Corporate Responsibility Magazine*) publishes this list annually. Detailed information on the methodology used to compile the list is available on the company website: http://www.thecro.com/.

[xviii]KPMG. 2011. International survey of corporate responsibility reporting 2011. Amsterdam: KPMG.

[xix]Committee for Economic Development. 1971. *Social responsibilities of business corporations.* New York: Author, see pgs. 15–16.

[xx]Carroll, A. B. 1991. The pyramid of corporate social responsibility: Toward the moral management of organizational stakeholders. *Business Horizons,* 34: 39–48.

[xxi]For a defense of this view, see Lockett, A., Moon, J., and Visser, W. 2006. Corporate social responsibility in management research: Focus, nature, salience and sources of influence. *Journal of Management Studies,* 43(1): 115–136; also see Crane, A., McWilliams, A., Matten, D., Moon, J., and Siegel, D. 2008. The corporate social responsibility agenda. In A. Crane, A. McWilliams, D. Matten, J. Moon, and D. Siegel (Eds.), *The Oxford handbook of corporate social responsibility:* 3–15. Oxford: Oxford University Press, pgs. 6–7.

[xxii]United Nations General Assembly. 1987. Report of the World Commission on Environment and Development: Our common future, pg. 16; http://www.un-documents.net/wced-ocf.htm.

[xxiii]Although the terms CSR and corporate citizenship may be used interchangeably in certain contexts, corporation citizenship is viewed by scholars as a distinct concept and is associated with its own stream of academic dialogue and research. The following papers provide a good introduction to the academic side of corporate citizenship: Matten, D. and Crane, A. 2005. Corporate citizenship: Toward an extended theoretical conceptualization. *Academy of Management Journal,* 30(1): 166–179; Moon, J., Crane, A., and Matten, D. 2005. Can corporations be citizens? Corporate citizenship as a metaphor for business participation in society. *Business Ethics Quarterly,* 15(3): 429–453; Néron, P.-Y. and Norman, W. 2008. Citizenship, Inc. Do we really want businesses to be good corporate citizens? *Business Ethics Quarterly,* 18(1): 1–26; Windsor, D. 2001. Corporate citizenship: Evolution and interpretation. In Andriof and McIntosh (Eds.), *Perspectives on corporate citizenship:* 39–52. Sheffield: Greenleaf; Wood, D. J. and Logsdon, J. M. 2008. Business citizenship as metaphor and reality. *Business Ethics Quarterly,* 18(1): 51–59.

[xxiv]For an introduction to corporate social performance, see Swanson, D. L. 1995. Addressing a theoretical problem by reorienting the corporate social performance model. *Academy of Management Review,* 20: 43–64; Swanson, D. L. 1999. Toward an integrative theory of business and society: A research strategy for corporate social performance. *Academy of Management Review,* 24(3): 506–521; Wood, D. J. 1991. Corporate social performance revisited. *Academy of Management Review,* 16(4): 691–718; Wood, D. J. 2010. Measuring corporate social performance: A review. *International Journal of Management Reviews,* 12(1): 50–84.

[xxv]For a good historical overview of the development and evolution of CSR, see Murphy, P. E. 1978. An evolution: Corporate social responsiveness. *University of Michigan Business Review,* 6(30): 19–25; Carroll, A. B. 1999. Corporate social responsibility: Evolution of a definitional construct. *Business and Society,* 38(3): 268–296; Carroll, A. B. 2008. A history of corporate social responsibility: Concepts and practices. In A. Crane, A. McWilliams, D. Matten, J. Moon, and D. Siegel (Eds.), *The Oxford handbook of corporate social responsibility:* 19–46. Oxford: Oxford University Press.

[xxvi]For a good introduction to stakeholder theory, see Freeman, R. E. 1984. *Strategic management: A stakeholder approach.* Boston: Pitman Publishing Inc.; Freeman, R. E. and Liedtka, J. 1991. Corporate social responsibility: A critical approach. *Business Horizons,* 34(4): 92–98; Freeman, R. E., Harrison, J., Parmar, B., and de Colle, S. 2010. *Stakeholder theory: The state of the art.* Cambridge, UK: Cambridge University Press.

[xxvii]Freeman, R. E. 1984. *Strategic management: A stakeholder approach.* Boston: Pitman Publishing Inc., pg. 25.

[xxviii]Freeman, R. E. and Velamuri, S. R. 2006. A new approach to CSR: Company stakeholder responsibility. In Kakabadse, A., and Morsing, M. (Eds.), *Corporate social responsibility: Reconciling aspiration with application:* 9–23. New York: Palgrave Macmillan.

[xxix]For a definition (and brief discussion) of subsistence or living wage, see http://en.wikipedia.org/wiki/Subsistence_wage.

[xxx]For a definition (and brief discussion) of social safety net programs, see http://en.wikipedia.org/wiki/Social_safety_net.

[xxxi]McGuire, J. W. 1963. *Business and society.* New York: McGraw-Hill Book Company, Inc., see page 144.

[xxxii]Davis, K. and Blomstrom, R. L. 1966. *Business and society: Environment and responsibility.* New York: McGraw-Hill, see page 7.

[xxxiii]Wood, D. J. 1991. Corporate social performance revisited. *Academy of Management Review,* 16(4): 691–718, see page 695.

[xxxiv]Holme, R. and Watts, P. 2000. *Corporate social responsibility: Making good business sense:* World Business Council for Sustainable Development, http://www.wbcsd.org/home.aspx.

[xxxv]Council on Foundations. 2012. *Increasing impact, enhancing value: A practitioner's guide to leading corporate philanthropy,* pg. 8, http://www.cof.org/.

[xxxvi]http://en.wikipedia.org/wiki/Corporate_social_responsibility, accessed on Feb. 6, 2013.

2

Three Foundational Assumptions

Isn't profit enough?

If businesses focus on earning an honest profit—where "honest" reflects a sincere commitment to "play by the rules"—isn't that enough? Why should businesses, in addition to striving to maximize profits, be expected to commit resources to addressing social and environmental issues, and then expend time and energy preparing both traditional financial statements and detailed corporate responsibility reports?

The short answer to the opening question is this: "No, in many cases, an honest profit isn't enough."

In this chapter, we lay the groundwork for an explanation of why this is the case by examining three important assumptions often made by CSR advocates:

Business and society overlap in important ways and are mutually dependent.

Economic markets are social institutions. In order for markets to function properly, a number of supporting institutions are required, and certain conditions must be met.

Societies expect certain outcomes from economic systems. If these outcomes aren't realized, then it's reasonable for societies to attempt to modify or change their economic systems so that these outcomes are obtained.

MUTUAL DEPENDENCE

In a 2006 article in the Harvard Business Review entitled "Strategy and Society: The Link Between Competitive Advantage and Corporate Social Responsibility," Michael E. Porter and Mark R. Kramer explain the relationship between business and society as follows:[i]

> Successful corporations need a healthy society. Education, health care, and equal opportunity are essential to a productive workforce. Safe products and working conditions not only attract customers but lower the internal costs of accidents. Efficient utilization of land, water, energy, and other natural resources makes business more productive. Good government, the rule of law, and property rights are essential for efficiency and innovation. Strong regulatory standards protect both consumers and competitive companies from exploitation. Ultimately, a healthy society creates expanding demand for business, as more human needs are met and aspirations grow. Any business that pursues its ends at the expense of the society in which it operates will find its success to be illusory and ultimately temporary.

> At the same time, a healthy society needs successful companies. No social program can rival the business sector when it comes to creating the jobs, wealth, and innovation that improve standards of living and social conditions over time. If governments, NGOs, and other participants in civil society weaken the ability of business to operate productively, they may win battles but will lose the war, as corporate and regional competitiveness fade, wages stagnate, jobs disappear, and the wealth that pays taxes and supports nonprofit contributions evaporates.

In addition to the mutual dependence that Porter and Kramer highlight, business and society are bound together in an even more fundamental way. The building blocks of society (e.g., language conventions, communication systems, shared understandings, behavioral norms, shared culture), are also the building blocks of business. In other words, businesses are built from the same raw materials as the larger social system in which they are embedded. While it is often claimed that businesses supply critical inputs to society (e.g., products and services of all kinds, employment, innovation), it is also true that society supplies businesses with equally critical inputs (e.g., an educated workforce, infrastructure, monetary system, police protection, access to courts).

In some circles, although there is begrudging acknowledgment of some degree of mutual dependence, it is often asserted that government and other social institutions are more dependent on the productive efforts of businesses than vice versa. For example, the following quote is from a leading textbook on strategic corporate social responsibility:

> Without the great wealth-producing engines of business, the taxes and charity needed to run government and non-profits fade away, in time reducing our standard of living to some primitive level. A simple thought experiment underscores these points: Look around you and subtract everything that was produced by a business. What is left? Or another example: What is the difference between the poorest nation and the wealthiest nation? Is it not primarily the creativity and productivity of businesses embedded in a societal-defined context?[ii]

A careful assessment of the relationship between business and society challenges this view in at least two ways. First, economic value creation is not the exclusive domain of business. Loosely defined, economic value creation is achieved by acquiring control over resources with a certain value, and then combining or transforming these resources to produce products and/or services with a greater value than the resources used to produce them. For example, the economic value created by the production of an iPhone is the difference between its final value and the total value of all resources utilized in its production. Similarly, if a community were to pool its resources and build a public library, subtracting the total value of utilized resources from the final value of the library would yield a measure of the economic value created.

Although there are important differences between business activities in economic markets and the production of goods and services through governmental or social efforts, recognizing that economic value can be created through either approach suggests that neither should be viewed as derivative of the other.

Familiarity with economic markets and private goods often makes it difficult to see the process of economic value creation independent of how it is managed or controlled (i.e., through economic markets, or through governmental or social processes). The following question illustrates this point: From the perspective of an average American citizen, in 2011, how does the economic value created by Microsoft compare to the economic value created by the U.S. military? For the full year ending on June 30, 2012, Microsoft generated a profit of around $17 billion on revenue of approximately $74 billion. The U.S. military, in contrast, contributed $820 billion to the U.S. GDP in 2011 (or 5.4%). The economic value created in each case can be derived by subtracting the value of all inputs from the value of all outputs. In Microsoft's case, total economic value created is probably close to double Microsoft's annual profit (assuming the average price of each transaction was halfway between supplier cost and the full value attributed to the product by the buyer). In the case of the U.S. military, total value created is equal to the sum of the value each individual in the U.S. places on what the military produces (e.g., national security, military supremacy) less the total value of all inputs. Assuming attributed value is 50% higher than the total inputs (a conservative estimate), the military generated approximately $400 billion in economic value (or approximately thirteen times the economic value created by Microsoft). Note that determining the value of end products, both in the market, and in the case of public goods, like national defense, is a subjective process that requires a number of assumptions. Regardless, the process of value creation is the same in economic markets as it is in governmental or social contexts. In each case, the amount of economic value created is derived by subtracting the value of all inputs from the value of all outputs.

Second, as Figure 2.1 illustrates, in addition to producing significant economic value, a number of critical business inputs are produced through governmental or social processes. Likewise, businesses, in addition to creating significant economic value, generate critical governmental and social inputs. The mutual dependence of government and market activity is illustrated by these two questions: "Could businesses or markets function without the critical inputs produced by governmental or social efforts? and "Could governmental or social efforts be effective without market inputs?" The answer to each of these questions is "no."

Based on Figure 2.1, the paragraph cited above asserting the primacy of market activity could be rewritten as follows:

> Without the critical inputs generated by collective or government efforts, including public goods such as national security, internal law and order, a system of property rights, access to courts, a monetary system, roads, airports, and other public infrastructure, public education, and regulatory efforts designed to constrain negative externalities and improve market functioning, economic markets would fade away and the value-creation efforts of business would become increasingly difficult. A simple thought experiment underscores this point: Look around you and subtract everything that was produced through governmental or social effort. Could businesses function without a monetary system, roads, an educated work force, and so on? Or another example: What is the difference between the poorest nations and the wealthiest nations? Is it not primarily the degree of law and order, safety and security, public infrastructure, and other public goods that make an efficient economic system possible?

MARKETS AS SOCIAL INSTITUTIONS

In addition to the idea that business and society are mutually dependent (see Figure 2.1), CSR advocates view economic markets as social institutions. From this perspective, markets are complex systems of social interaction that must be carefully structured and

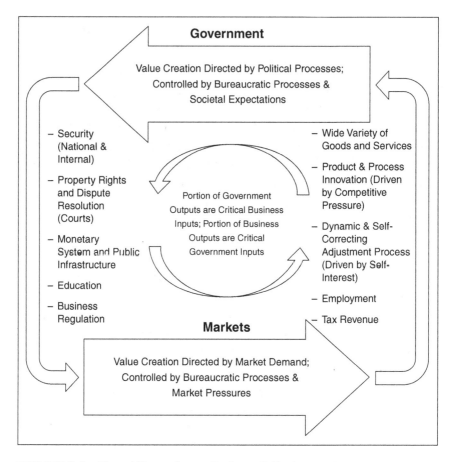

FIGURE 2.1 Mutual Dependence: Business & Government

maintained. To operate efficiently, markets require a mix of shared norms, enforceable rules, and supporting institutions. In almost all cases, public goods are necessary. Charles E. Lindblom, in his book entitled *The Market System: What It Is, How It Works, and What to Make of It,* identifies eight supporting institutions required by market systems: 1) Customs and laws that facilitate the exercise of personal liberty, 2) A stable system of broad property rights, 3) Customs and laws that make quid pro quo the primary basis of exchange (and therefore prohibit the use of violence or theft to obtain property), 4) A medium of exchange or money, 5) A societal shift from work within the household to the sale of objects and performances outside the household, 6) The emergence of economic intermediaries (i.e., market makers), 7) The emergence of entrepreneurs who specialize in establishing exchange linkages and exploiting market opportunities, and 8) The emergence of collectives that can operate on a capital and coordination scale that individuals cannot.[iii]

In addition to the supporting institutions identified by Lindblom, if economic markets are to yield optimal outcomes, certain structural conditions must be met, such as large numbers of buyers and sellers, each fully informed and acting independently.[iv] If these conditions are met, or at least reasonably approximated, the behavior of market participants will be constrained and channeled by competitive pressure. Constant competitive jockeying will result in the lowest price possible for a given product or service, which will ensure that the largest quantity possible is produced and consumed.

Because the emergence of supporting social institutions and the necessary conditions for efficient market functioning are unlikely to occur spontaneously, market systems should not be thought of as naturally-occurring social phenomena. Barter-based exchanges may emerge in the course of ongoing social interaction, but such exchanges are as far removed from market systems as playing catch with a football in one's backyard is from the National Football League. Bridging the gap between barter-based economic exchanges and market-based economic systems requires intentional societal intervention. Learning to establish and maintain efficient economic markets, in many ways, is one of the most impressive social achievements of modern civilization.

Although business and society may be mutually dependent in the sense that each produces key inputs required by the other (see Figure 2.1), in systemic terms, there is a clear hierarchy: Markets are defined and structured by society. As ongoing work in economic sociology—a field that focuses on the social causes and effects of different economic phenomena—demonstrates, the most efficient markets are often the most structured in terms of norms, codes of conduct, policies, and enforcement protocols. For example, the New York Stock Exchange is a carefully structured exchange environment with a long history of norms, precedents, policies, and rules.[v]

Although markets are a versatile, robust, and effective form of economic organization, there are situations in which the necessary conditions for efficient markets cannot be met. In some cases, for example, product characteristics or the structure of the market itself may prevent proper market functioning.[vi] In these cases, society may take steps to constrain or direct business behavior in order to improve outcomes. The role of CSR in these contexts is explored further in Chapter 3. Here it is sufficient to observe that societal intervention in these situations illustrates the hierarchical relationship between business and society; it is society that defines and structures the economic space in which businesses operate—not the other way around.

SOCIAL CONTROL

From a CSR perspective, economic systems are a means to an end. In other words, societies set up economic systems with the expectation of achieving certain outcomes. If these outcomes are not realized, societies may elect to alter or change their economic systems. Although CSR advocates may acknowledge the mutual dependence of business and society, they do not view it as an equal partnership. Business is a part of society and therefore subject to societal control. There is often open hostility to the notion that society should be correspondingly subject to corporate control.[vii]

Although the social control of economic activity is important to a broad understanding of CSR, it is, nonetheless, an abstraction that can be difficult for firms to incorporate into their day-to-day decision making. Two concepts help bridge this gap—license to operate, and the iron law of responsibility.

License to Operate

Historically, the term "license to operate" has referred to situations in which firms or industries operated in areas controlled by indigenous people.[viii] In these cases, it is important that indigenous communities or populations be consulted and give their informed consent. In practical terms, this implies that firms must actively engage with indigenous populations and make sure that interactions are mutually beneficial. This is particularly important in extractive industries, such as mining, or oil and gas drilling. For example, Meridian Gold, a Nevada-based company, was recently forced to abandon a mine in Argentina and to take a write-down of nearly $400 million on the property because it failed to secure prior permission from local communities.[ix]

The term "license to operate" is now used to refer, in a general way, to the notion that firms should be cognizant of the level of support they enjoy in the communities and societies in which they operate. In practical terms, the greater the level of trust and support firms enjoy, the less likely they will be subjected to burdensome regulation. In this sense, "license to operate" is often used to refer to the idea that businesses should voluntarily comply with societal expectations in order to preserve their ability (or "license") to direct their own affairs. In cases in which firms fail to comply with societal expectations, this freedom (or "license") may be suspended or revoked. In other words, failure to voluntarily comply with societal expectations may result in firms being forced through regulatory and/or legal means to do so. In general, businesses are likely to prefer the former arrangement to the latter.[x]

Iron Law of Responsibility

The Iron Law of Responsibility, although similar to the notion of a license to operate, focuses more on the link between power and responsibility than the threat of regulation. This law can be expressed as follows: "In the long run, those who do not use power in a manner in which society considers responsible will tend to lose it."[xi]

The Iron Law of Responsibility is often referenced as one of the primary reasons why businesses should be careful to respond to changing societal norms and expectations. If businesses do not respond to changes in societal expectations, then the Iron Law of Responsibility suggests that over time, the responsibility and power now enjoyed by the business community will diminish. Keith Davis, in an influential article published in 1960, explained it this way:

But what are the consequences of responsibility avoidance? If power and responsibility are to be relatively equal, then the avoidance of social responsibility leads to gradual erosion of social power. To the extent that businessmen [or businesswomen] do not accept social-responsibility opportunities as they arise, other groups will step in to assume these responsibilities. Historically, government and labor have been most active in the role of diluting business power, and probably they will continue to be the principal challenging groups. I am not proposing that this should happen, but on the basis of the evidence, it appears that this will tend to happen to the extent that businessmen do not keep their social responsibilities approximately equal with their social power.[xii]

The Iron Law of Responsibility draws attention to the important role that business has often played in societal evolution and development. To the degree that business continues to be perceived as a trustworthy advocate of societal interests, it will retain its current level of power and influence. On the other hand, if business is perceived to be promoting its own interest at the expense of broader society, its power and influence will almost certainly erode.

The mutual dependence of business and government, the fact that markets are social institutions, and the legitimacy of societal control of economic activity are often assumed in CSR contexts. Understanding these assumptions is important groundwork for understanding why, in many cases, a focus on profit is not enough to ensure that the actions of market participants will promote societal interests.

CHAPTER SUMMARY

In many cases, a focus on profit isn't enough to ensure that the actions of market participants will serve societal interests. As a foundation for understanding why this is the case, it is important to understand three important assumptions often made by CSR advocates.

First, business and society overlap in important ways. Economic value can be created through market activity as well as through governmental or social processes. These different approaches to value creation are mutually dependent. For example, it would be difficult for businesses to operate without security, property rights, a monetary system, public infrastructure, and regulatory oversight. Likewise, it would be difficult for government to function without inputs derived from the productive efforts of businesses.

Second, markets are social institutions. To operate efficiently, they require a mix of shared norms, enforceable rules, supporting institutions and public goods. In addition, certain structural conditions must be met, such as a large number of buyers and sellers. In some cases, however, product characteristics or the structure of the market itself may prevent proper market functioning. In these cases, intervention may be necessary to promote societal interests.

Finally, from a CSR perspective, societies set up economic systems with the expectation of achieving certain outcomes. If these outcomes aren't realized, then societies may elect to alter or change their economic systems. Social control of economic systems is explicitly reflected in two important concepts—license to operate, and the Iron Law of Responsibility.

REVIEW QUESTIONS

1. How are business and society mutually dependent? Provide some specific examples.

2. Why shouldn't markets be thought of as naturally-occurring phenomena? What supporting social institutions do markets require?

3. Explain this statement: "From a CSR perspective, economic systems are a means to an end."

4. What is "license to operate?" What is the Iron Law of Responsibility? How are they similar? How are they different?

ENDNOTES

[i] See Porter, M. E. and Kramer, M. R. 2006. Strategy & society: The link between competitive advantage and corporate social responsibility. *Harvard Business Review*, 84(12): 78–92, page 83.

[ii] Werther, W. B. and Chandler, D. 2011. *Strategic corporate social responsibility: Stakeholders in a global environment*. Thousand Oaks, CA: SAGE Publications, Inc., pg. xxiii.

[iii]See Lindblom, C. E. 2001. *The market system: What it is, how it works, and what to make of it.* New Haven: Yale University Press, particularly Chapter 4, pages 52–60.

[iv]For an accessible, but thorough, discussion of the perfect competition market model, see Chapter 2 of Walters, S. J. K. 1993. *Enterprise, government, and the public.* New York: McGraw-Hill. For a more advanced treatment of the same, see Bator, F. M. 1957. The simple analytics of welfare maximization. *American Economic Review*, 47(1): 22–59, and Bator, F. M. 1958. The anatomy of market failure. *The Quarterly Journal of Economics*, 72(3): 351–379.

[v]Fligstein, N. 2001. *The architecture of markets: An economic sociology of twenty-first century capitalist societies.* Princeton: Princeton University Press.

[vi]Stiglitz, J. E. 2000. *Economics of the public sector* (3rd ed.). New York: W. W. Norton & Company; Pepall, L., Richards, D. J., and Norman, G. 2005. *Industrial organization: Contemporary theory and practice* (3rd ed.). Mason, OH: South-Western; For a thorough popular press treatment of market failure, see Cassidy, J. 2009. *How markets fail: The logic of economic calamities.* New York: Farrar, Straus and Giroux, particularly Chapter 10.

[vii]For an interesting discussion of corporate social responsibility and economic ideology, see Scherer, A. G. and Palazzo, G. 2007. Toward a political conception of corporate social responsibility: Business and society seen from a Habermasian perspective. *Academy of Management Review*, 32(4): 1096–1120.

[viii]For a discussion of the evolution of the phrase "license to operate," see Wilburn, K. M. and Wilburn, R. 2011. Achieving social license to operate using stakeholder theory. *Journal of International Business Ethics*, 4(2): 3–16; The Declaration on the Rights of Indigenous Peoples, passed by the United Nations in 2007, can be found here: http://social.un.org/index/IndigenousPeoples/DeclarationontheRightsofIndigenousPeoples.aspx.

[ix]Wilburn, K. M. and Wilburn, R. 2011. Achieving social license to operate using stakeholder theory. *Journal of International Business Ethics*, 4(2): 3–16.

[x]See Breitbarth, T., Harris, P., and Aitken, R. 2009. Corporate social responsibility in the European Union: A new trade barrier? *Journal of Public Affairs*, 9(4): 239–255; Porter, M. E. and Kramer, M. R. 2006. Strategy & society: The link between competitive advantage and corporate social responsibility. *Harvard Business Review*, 84(12): 78–92; Zinkin, J. 2004. Maximising the 'licence to operate.' *Journal of Corporate Citizenship*(14): 67–80.

[xi]See Davis, K. and Blomstrom, R. L. 1975. *Business and society: Environment and responsibility* (3rd ed.). New York: McGraw-Hill, pg. 50. See also Davis, K. 1960. Can business afford to ignore social responsibilities? *California Management Review*, 2: 70–76 and Davis, K. 1973. The case for and against business assumption of social responsibilities. *Academy of Management Journal*, 16(2): 312–322.

[xii]See Davis, K. 1960. Can business afford to ignore social responsibilities? *California Management Review*, 2: 70–76, page 73.

3

CSR and Value Creation

WHAT DO WE WANT?

As a society, what, exactly, do we want from our economic system? Because CSR is generally defined in terms that link the behavior of individual businesses to macroeconomic outcomes (see Chapter 1), this question anchors CSR in much the same way that vision or mission statements anchor the strategies of individual firms. The first step in making CSR relevant for individual firms, therefore, is to make these objectives explicit.

In his 1953 book, *Social Responsibilities of the Businessman*, Bowen lists eleven macroeconomic objectives: high standard of living, economic progress, economic stability, personal security, order, justice, freedom, development of the individual person, community improvement, national security, and personal integrity.[i]

In their 1966 textbook on the relationship between business and society, Keith Davis and Robert Blomstrom list the following areas of potential social involvement: ecology and environmental quality, consumerism, community needs, governmental relations, business giving, minorities and disadvantaged persons, labor relations, stockholder relations, and economic activities.[ii]

These lists remain relevant more than fifty years later. For example, during the 2012 U.S. presidential debates between Barack

Obama, the incumbent and Democratic nominee, and Mitt Romney, the Republican nominee, nearly every item on these lists was addressed as each candidate attempted to communicate his respective aspirations for the U.S. economy. Although there may be disagreement regarding specific items, these objectives nevertheless serve to anchor the concept of CSR. As observed in Chapter 1, at the heart of CSR is the notion that individual firms have a responsibility to behave in a manner that contributes to the realization of desired economic outcomes. These lists represent a laudable attempt to make these outcomes explicit.

HOW DO WE GET THERE?

Even though there may be general consensus about what we want from our economic system, there is still significant debate over the means of getting there. This is because it is often difficult to determine what participants in our economic system should do in order to produce the outcomes we want. The following scenario illustrates why making this determination can often be difficult.

Imagine that fire has just erupted in a crowded theater with only one narrow exit. Furthermore, assume that everyone in the crowd is able to immediately assess the situation; if the crowd exits as quickly as possible, seventy-five percent of those in the theater will survive. Assuming everyone is committed to the best outcome for the group—a seventy-five percent survival rate—what should each individual do? Because the exit is narrow, movement of the crowd will resemble the movement of sand through an hourglass. Like the sand at the top of the hourglass, at the back of the crowd, movement will be almost indiscernible. As individuals in the crowd move forward, however, the width of the group will narrow and movement toward the door will accelerate. Even though the group objective is to exit as quickly as possible, the most effective way for the individuals in the back to contribute to a rapid exit is to move slowly towards the exit, being careful to avoid jostling or pushing individuals in front of them.

For those in the back of the crowd, moving slowly towards the exit may seem like a counterintuitive way to increase the speed at which the group is able to exit. If those in the back attempt to move more quickly, however, individuals will fall down (or be pushed to the ground), and chaos will ensue. This will slow the group down and fewer people will escape. For those in the back of the theater, however, because not everyone will be able to exit, contributing to an orderly exit by moving slowing reduces the odds of their survival to zero. This creates a critical divergence between what is in the best interests of those individuals in the back of the theater, and what is in the best interest of the group. They can improve their individual odds by attempting to move more quickly, but by doing so they will induce panic and thereby reduce the group's overall rate of exit. We will revisit the issue of divergent incentives later in this chapter.

The same counterintuitive relationship between individual behavior and group or collective outcomes exists in economic markets. In properly functioning markets, it is assumed that self-interested behavior by participants will produce optimal macroeconomic outcomes. As Adam Smith observed of a representative market participant, "by pursuing his own interest he frequently promotes that of the society more effectually than when he really intends to promote it."[iii] John Maynard Keynes is reported to have stated the same idea this way: "Capitalism is the astounding belief that the most wickedest of men will do the most wickedest of things for the greatest good of everyone."[iv] Just as moving slowly in the fire scenario described earlier counterintuitively contributes to the speed at which the group is able to exit, in the case of economic markets, working to promote one's own interests is often the most effective way to contribute to collective or societal interests. It is important to note, however, that although the links between individual behavior and group or system outcomes are counterintuitive in both instances, in the case of economic markets, there is an alignment of individual and group interests (i.e., what is in the best interest of the individual is also in the best interest of the group). In the fire scenario, in contrast, there is a divergence between individual and group interests.

As these examples illustrate, the link between participant behavior and system outcomes is often difficult to predict. In early research on crowd behavior, it was often mistakenly assumed that the characteristics of aggregate behavior were indicative of the character of the behavior of individual participants. If observed crowd behavior was erratic, emotional or irrational, for example, then it was assumed that the behavior of individuals in the crowd was also erratic, emotional or irrational. Subsequent analysis revealed that these early assumptions were mistaken. Rational individual behavior can produce collectively irrational behavior—a situation often referred to as "collective irrationality."[v] This can be seen clearly in the theater fire example. Rational behavior by individuals in the back of the crowd—attempting to move more quickly to the exit, and thereby increasing their own odds of survival—would produce a collectively irrational outcome (i.e., a suboptimal exit rate for the group).

From a CSR perspective, establishing a clear link between individual behavior and group or system outcomes is essential. In contrast to the invisible hand of economic markets, CSR asks businesses to explicitly consider societal expectations with regard to specific macroeconomic outcomes, and to then regulate their behavior in order to satisfy these expectations. Unless businesses are able to establish a reliable link between their behavior and these outcomes, businesses cannot be expected to effectively contribute to their realization.

Market theory is often the default method of linking business behavior to macroeconomic outcomes. It is unfortunate that CSR is often viewed as separate from—or in some cases, antagonistic towards—traditional market-based activities. This is understandable, however, given that CSR efforts are often motivated by a desire to mitigate market deficiencies. On the other hand, establishing links between business behavior and macroeconomic outcomes is critical to CSR, and market theory represents a well-developed and empirically-tested framework for reliably establishing these links. In situations in which markets are dysfunctional or absent, other methods are needed. One of the potential contributions of scholarly CSR dialogue is the development of alternative frameworks that can be applied in these situations.

The question "How do we get there?" was posed at the start of this section. Stated more formally: Assuming we know what we want from our economic system, what should system participants do to contribute to the outcomes we want? The remainder of this chapter focuses on different ways of linking business behavior to macroeconomic outcomes. Even though there may be broad consensus regarding the macroeconomic outcomes we want, there is still likely to be considerable debate about the most effective means of realizing these outcomes. As you read the remainder of the chapter, consider why this is the case.

THE PERFECT
COMPETITION MARKET MODEL

As one prominent author asserts, "the ideal of a free, self-regulating market is newly triumphant . . . unfettered markets are deemed both the essence of human liberty, and the most expedient route to prosperity."[vi] Popular understanding of how markets function is captured in the perfect competition market model (PCMM). The PCMM is a simplified model of economic markets that satisfies a number of important conditions, including a large number of buyers and sellers, fully-informed participants, and the free movement of productive resources. The PCMM is the quintessential economic market—decentralized, self-regulating, and fiercely competitive.

The logic of the PCMM is straightforward. There must be a large number of independent buyers and sellers. No market participants can have the ability to affect market prices, and products must be interchangeable (i.e., homogenous). There can be no barriers to entry or exit, no artificial restraints on prices, and all participants must be fully informed.[vii] If these conditions are met, then the profit motive ensures that firms that supply goods and/or services will closely monitor their costs and will do everything within their power to increase efficiency and minimize waste. In addition, firms will also strive to accurately determine their optimal level of output, based on the prices of inputs, their own production function, and the market price of the good or service in question. If they produce too little, they surrender potential profit. If they produce too much, the firm is responsible for the associated losses. The process of determining how much of a particular good or service to supply makes companies sensitive to price fluctuations. For example, an increase in market price may induce a company to significantly increase production. In contrast, an increase in the price of a key input may induce a company to significantly reduce production. Competitive pressure, therefore, creates powerful incentive for companies to not only produce goods and services efficiently, but to also produce them in the right quantities.

Because products in a particular market are interchangeable, intense competition forces companies to strive to offer consumers a superior value proposition. Competitive jockeying results in the lowest possible market price, and this ensures that the largest possible quantity is demanded and exchanged. This, in turn, results in the greatest amount of subjective economic well-being. In the precise language of economists, efficient markets lead to productive and allocative efficiency (i.e., goods and services will be produced efficiently, and in the appropriate quantities), and to the maximization of social surplus (i.e., economic well-being will be maximized). [viii]

It is important to recognize that the PCMM explicitly links individual behavior and macroeconomic outcomes. It is assumed that if businesses are motivated by a desire to maximize profit, their behavior will lead to productive and allocative efficiency, and the maximization of social surplus. In the context of the PCMM, therefore, it follows that if businesses want to contribute to the realization of these outcomes—as CSR suggests they should—then businesses should seek to maximize profit.

The Friedman Doctrine

In 1970, Milton Friedman, an economist and recipient of the Nobel Prize in Economics, authored a short article in the *New York Times* in which he articulated a view of CSR that has become known as the "Friedman Doctrine."[ix] This doctrine asserts that the primary social responsibility of a business is to increase its profits. The following paragraphs are excerpted from Friedman's *New York Times* article:

> What does it mean to say that the corporate executive has a "social responsibility" in his capacity as businessman? If this statement is not pure rhetoric, it must mean that he is to act in some way that is not in the interest of his employers. For example, that he is to refrain from increasing the price of the product in order to contribute to the social objective of preventing inflation, even though a price increase

would be in the best interests of the corporation. Or that he is to make expenditures on reducing pollution beyond the amount that is in the best interests of the corporation or that is required by law in order to contribute to the social objective of improving the environment. Or that, at the expense of corpórate profits, he is to hire "hardcore" unemployed instead of better qualified available workmen to contribute to the social objective of reducing poverty. In each of these cases, the corporate executive would be spending someone else's money for a general social interest. Insofar as his actions in accord with his "social responsibility" reduce returns to stockholders, he is spending their money. Insofar as his actions raise the price to customers, he is spending the customers' money. Insofar as his actions lower the wages of some employees, he is spending their money.

. . . .

But the doctrine of "social responsibility" taken seriously would extend the scope of the political mechanism to every human activity. It does not differ in philosophy from the most explicitly collective doctrine. It differs only by professing to believe that collectivist ends can be attained without collectivist means. That is why, in my book *Capitalism and Freedom*, I have called it a "fundamentally subversive doctrine" in a free society, and have said that in such a society, "there is one and only one social responsibility of business—to use its resources and engage in activities designed to increase its profits so long as it stays within the rules of the game, which is to say, engages in open and free competition without deception or fraud." [x]

Friedman's assertion that "there is one and only one social responsibility of business—to use its resources and engage in activities designed to increase its profits" is often cited by CSR critics to justify a focus on profit maximization based exclusively on financial accounting.

For Friedman, the primary manifestation of CSR during the time he wrote this article was what he perceived as growing pressure to obligate businesses to engage in charitable efforts to solve persistent social problems, such as underemployment or poverty. Friedman viewed this pressure as an attempt to appropriate private property (i.e., business assets) for public purposes. Friedman viewed this as an alarming erosion of private property rights and therefore asserted that CSR was a "fundamentally subversive doctrine" (Friedman, 1970: 2)[xi]

It is important to recognize that Friedman's concept of CSR as a kind of obligatory philanthropy is different in a number of significant respects than a view of CSR that emphasizes the link between the actions of individual businesses and outcomes for which they—considered as a group—are directly responsible. Friedman may have been correct to assert that obligating businesses to address enduring social ills for which they have no direct responsibility would fundamentally alter the DNA of market-based economies. This position, however, is only tangentially related to the assertion of contemporary CSR advocates that businesses have a responsibility to consider the link between their individual actions and associated group or system outcomes that satisfy societal expectations. If Friedman's assertion that businesses should stay within the "rules of the game" is interpreted as an admonition for businesses to conform to societal expectations in this respect, then Friedman's position is more supportive of a contemporary understanding of CSR than critics generally acknowledge.

ALTERNATIVE FRAMEWORKS

Although the PCMM reflects common understanding of economic markets, it is not the only method of connecting individual behavior to group or system outcomes. Markets require a number of supporting institutions and must satisfy a number of conditions if they are to deliver optimal outcomes. The term "market failure" is used to describe situations in which markets fail to function properly.[xii] As demonstrated by the financial crisis of 2007–2008—the worst economic crisis in the U.S. since the Great Depression in the 1930s—in some cases, market failure can be catastrophic.[xiii] In situations in which market failure is likely, government or social action can often produce superior outcomes.

From a CSR perspective, it is important that businesses understand when the pursuit of profit is likely to contribute to the social good, and when it is unlikely to do so. Market failure explanations are similar to the PCMM in the sense that they link individual behavior to specific group or system outcomes. In contrast to the PCMM, however, a market failure approach connects individual behavior to inefficient or undesirable outcomes.

Social dilemmas, defined as "interaction situations in which rational individual behavior produces irrational group or collective outcomes" represent another method of connecting individual behavior and group or system outcomes.[xiv] Social dilemmas, in contrast to both the PCMM and market failure, focuses on situations in which the incentives or payoff for each individual are dependent on the actions of other participants. In these situations, the link between participant behavior and system outcomes is often counterintuitive (e.g., the fire scenario used earlier in the chapter), and self-interested behavior (i.e., "profit maximizing" behavior) will often lead negative group outcomes.

Market Failure

Market failure, as defined by one of the first economists to use the term, is "the failure of a more or less idealized system of price-market institutions to sustain 'desirable' activities or to estop 'undesirable' activities."[xv] Stated simply, market failure occurs when markets fail to deliver efficient outcomes. Market failure is likely when there are 1) externalities or spillover effects, 2) public goods, or 3) monopolies or oligopolies, natural monopolies, network externalities, information problems, or other structural idiosyncrasies that impede competition or create other incentive problems (see Table 3.1).

An *externality*, or *transaction spillover*, is a cost or a benefit that is not reflected in the price of a product that affects an unrelated third party. Environmental pollution is an example of a negative externality. If the manufacturing process associated with a particular product or service, for example, were to result in a significant amount of pollution, but the cost of this pollution were not

TABLE 3.1 Types of Market Failure

Causes	Problem Description	Example(s)
Externalities	Costs or benefits that are not reflected in the price of a product that affect unrelated third parties lead to over-supply or undersupply.	pollution (negative); LoJack (positive)
Production of Public Goods	Free-rider problems created by goods that are non-rivalrous (consumption does not decrease their availability) and non-excludable (benefits are difficult to restrict to those who contribute to their production) lead to undersupply.	national defense
Monopolies & Oligopolies	Insufficient competitive pressure results in insufficient efficiency incentives and prices that are too high to maximize overall economic value.	any market controlled by one or a small number of companies (movie studios, cell phone service providers, beer industry)
Natural Monopolies	Economies of scale over the entire demand range lead to higher prices because dividing up demand among competitors results in higher production costs for individual firms.	cable TV service
Network Externalities	When a significant portion of the value of a product is determined by the number of other users, competition will lead to market dominance by a single firm (see monopoly). The same dynamics can lead to the "lock-in" of inefficient standards.	telephone service; eBay; Facebook; the QWERTY keyboard (standard)

TABLE 3.1 Continued

Causes	Problem Description	Example(s)
Information Problems	Information asymmetries create adverse selection problems that make it difficult for parties to engage in mutually beneficial exchange.	health insurance
Structural Idiosyncrasies	Idiosyncratic features of particular markets complicate or prevent competition or insulate companies from competitive pressure, and this leads to insufficient efficiency incentives and prices that are too high to maximize overall economic value.	college textbooks, credit cards

reflected in the price of the product, then the price of this product would not accurately represent the value of the resources required to produce it. As a consequence, the product would be priced too low, and more than the optimal amount of the product would be demanded. On the other hand, if there were positive externalities associated with a particular product, but the price buyers were willing to pay for it failed to reflect the value of these benefits, then the market price would be too low, and too little of the product would be supplied.

The LoJack Stolen Vehicle Recovery System is an interesting example of a product with positive externalities. Installation of the LoJack security system involves hiding a small radio transceiver in a vehicle. If the vehicle is stolen, this transceiver can be activated, and police can use the signal to locate it. LoJack acts as a general deterrent to auto thieves because it enables police to locate chop shops and significantly increases the likelihood of arrest and prosecution. Because there is no obvious indication that a Lojack transceiver has been installed in a vehicle, the security system does little to prevent theft, and only a small portion of these benefits, therefore, are captured by individual LoJack customers. Because there is no ready buyer for the positive externalities generated by the device, less than the optimal level of LoJack systems are demanded. Researchers have estimated that for every $100 spent on LoJack security systems as much as $1500 of social benefits are generated, primarily in the form of reduced auto thefts. Because these benefits are "socialized" in a sense (i.e., they are spread indiscriminately across a community), these benefits are not reflected in private demand for the product, and these potential benefits are forfeited. The underprovision of goods and services with positive externalities by the market is a predictable and well-understood phenomenon.[xvi]

The significance of externalities, or transaction spillovers, has been debated by economists for more than a century. Arthur Cecil Pigou, in a book published in 1920 entitled *The Economics of Welfare*, argued that the presence of spillovers justified societal intervention in economic markets. Pigou's logic was persuasive. Economic markets, because they involve private transactions based on private costs and benefits, are unable to account for third party effects or spillovers (either positive or negative). Neither social costs nor social benefits will be represented in the calculus of the market, and this deficiency, if left uncorrected, will lead to the overproduction of goods associated with negative spillovers, and the underproduction of goods associated with positive spillovers.

The influence of Pigou's arguments were eventually muted by Ronald Coase, who argued in a 1960 paper entitled "The Problem of Social Cost," that spillovers could be resolved through the judicious assignment of property rights. For example, if a property owner were negatively affected by waste from a nearby manufacturing plant, assuming property rights were sufficiently defined and enforceable, this owner would be able to demand payment from the plant. The plant, because it would be forced to deal with the land owner, would then be forced to include the costs of disposing of its waste in the price of its products. In practice, however, difficulties assessing spillovers, the complex nature of property rights, and the costs of negotiation often make property rights solutions to spillovers impractical. Coase, in his 1991 Nobel Prize lecture, acknowledged that the costs of spillover detection, assessment, and then subsequent negotiation—costs that economists refer to as transaction costs—might make a collective (or government) solution more efficient:

Of course, it does not imply, when transaction costs are positive, that government actions (such as government operation, regulation or taxation, including subsidies) could not produce a better result than relying on negotiations between individuals in the market. Whether this would be so could be discovered not by studying imaginary governments but what real governments actually do. My conclusion; let us study the world of positive transaction costs.[xvii]

A *public good* is defined by two important characteristics: a) consumption does not decrease its availability to others, and b) benefits are difficult to restrict to those who contributed to its production. A common example of a public good is the safety and security afforded to a country by its military. Once resources are dedicated to a nation's defense, the enjoyment of that defense by one citizen does not decrease its availability to other citizens. Likewise, it is difficult to restrict the benefits of safety and security to contributing citizens. In economic terms, national defense is a good that is both non-rival (individual consumptions doesn't diminish its availability) and non-excludable (once produced, it is difficult to limit its consumption to just those that contributed to its production).

Public goods are likely to be chronically undersupplied by economic markets. Because public goods are non-rival and non-excludable, and non-contributors will derive as much benefit from their production as contributors, individuals have little incentive to contribute to their production. Furthermore, individuals are also likely to worry that if they do contribute, they will be taken advantage of by others who refuse to do so, intending to subsequently "free-ride" on their contributions. The temptation to free-ride, and wariness of the possibility that others will succumb to the temptation to do so, creates an incentive to refrain from contributing. In situations in which public goods are involved, even though significant economic value might be created by their production, they may fail to be produced.

When there is only one supplier of a particular good or service (*monopoly*), or a small number of suppliers (*oligopoly*), firms will face little competitive pressure, and will therefore have little incentive to focus on efficient production, optimal allocation, or to price their goods competitively in order to maximize overall economic value.[xviii] Examples of oligopolies in the U.S. include movie studios (the "big six," Columbia Pictures, Warner Bros., Walt Disney, Universal Picture, 20th Century Fox and Paramount Pictures, control approximately 90% of the motion picture market), the cellular service providers (AT&T Mobility, Verizon, T-Mobile and Sprint control approximately 90% of the cell phone service market), and the beer industry (Anheuser-Busch and MillerCoors have a combined industry market share of approximately 80%).

In some situations, however, it may not make sense to have more than one firm supply a given product or service. If, for example, there are significant economies of scale over the entire range of total demand for a product, then dividing up demand among a number of firms may result in significantly higher prices than if a single firm controlled the entire market. These situations are referred to as *natural monopolies*. The provision of cable TV service in a particular geographic area often exhibits the characteristics of a natural monopoly. The cost of providing this service may be $150/month if a firm services 10,000 households, but this cost may drop to $50/month if the number of subscribers is increased to 50,000. In a town in which there may be a total of 50,000 potential subscribers, dividing up this potential demand equally among five different companies, in order to insure some level of competition, may result in cable prices that are significantly higher than if just one cable company were allowed to operate in the market.

Network externalities (or *network effects*) are present when a significant portion of the value of a product or service to an individual is determined by the number of other users. The value of telephone service, for example, increases in lock-step with the number of telephone users. Other products characterized by strong network effects include computer operating systems, online auction sites, like eBay, or social media sites, like Twitter or Facebook. In the case of eBay, a significant portion of the value of its service to vendors is derived from the level of buyer traffic on its site. eBay is able to sustain this level of buyer traffic because its large number of vendors make it a convenient place to shop. This kind of positive feedback loop—an increase in the number of vendors leads to more buyers, and more buyers, in turn, leads to more vendors—often leads to market dominance by a single firm.

In situations in which a technological standard exhibits network effects, the result may be a situation in which an inefficient standard becomes impossible to dislodge, even in situations in which new products are clearly more efficient. The QWERTY keyboard is a classic example of this kind of technological "lock-in." The QWERTY keyboard was originally designed to optimize the mechanical functioning of early typewriters. Because individual letters were linked to metal arms or typebars, the letters commonly used in combination, like "st" or "th" were intentionally separated in order to prevent jams. Given that these mechanical constraints are no longer a concern, more efficient layouts are possible. One such layout, the Dvorak keyboard, requires less finger motion, and is therefore associated with fewer errors and higher typing speeds. If this keyboard were to become the standard, the efficiency gains from increased levels of keyboard productivity would be substantial. However, given that a significant portion of the value of the QWERTY keyboard lies in the fact that other individuals use it, there is insufficient incentive for individuals to switch to the new standard. Even though everyone would benefit from a move to a more efficient standard, because of the incentives created by existing network effects, the only way to make the move would be for individuals to band together and decide to do so en masse. The organizing costs associated with this kind of collective action are substantial, and have to date prevented such a move.[xix]

There are situations in which parties to a potential transaction have different information, and this asymmetry may prevent proper market functioning.[xx] For example, *information asymmetries* in the health insurance market complicate the sale of healthcare plans to individuals. If an insurance company were to actively market a healthcare plan for $500/month to the general public, individuals that anticipate medical expenses of more than $500/month would be the most likely to purchase it. This would result in a pool of insured individuals that would likely cost more than $500/month to insure, and the company would be forced to raise the price of its plan. This would cause plan participants to reevaluate whether or not the plan were still a "good deal" by comparing the new price of the plan to their expected medical expenses. This would likely result in the healthiest individuals in the pool dropping the plan, given that these individual would be the most likely to conclude that the new price exceeded expected expenses. This process would produce a smaller, but equally unprofitable, pool of insured individuals. This would again force the insurance company to raise the price of its plan, and the cycle would continue. This process—known as adverse selection—is one of the primary reasons that health insurance is generally sold to groups of individuals rather than directly to individuals.

Finally, there are situations in which markets are structured in a way that prevents competition from having the desired effect on supplier behavior. This is the case in the college textbook market. In this market, the buying decision (the "adoption" decision) is made by one party (the institution or professor), but the cost of the product is born by the student. The decision to adopt a particular textbook, therefore, is based on the preferences of the institution or professor, and is generally based on criteria other than price, such as the availability and quality of ancillary materials, authorial reputation, convenience, and so on. Competition to enhance these features (in order to increase the likelihood of adoption) drives up the price of textbooks. In other words, competitive pressure in the college textbook market drives prices up, not down. The credit card market is another context in which structural features prevent proper market functioning. In this case, credit card companies have been able to contractually require businesses to shield customers from the actual costs of using a credit card. This prevents customers from deciding which card to use based on the associated transaction expense (and this effectually insulates credit card companies from price-based competition).[xxi]

Social Dilemmas

Consider the scenario of a fire in a crowded theater presented earlier in this chapter. In this scenario, it is in the best interests of the group—considered collectively—to exit as quickly as possible; this implies that individuals should exit quickly, but in an orderly manner. From an individual perspective, however, pushing, shoving, and running for the exit is a superior strategy. To see this, consider the possible outcomes. If the crowd remains calm, running for the exit will increase one's odds of survival. Likewise, if the crowd panics, running will also increase one's odds of survival. Regardless of whether the crowd panics or not, from the perspective of an individual in the crowd, running always yields better survival odds. Unfortunately, if every individual approaches the dilemma in the same way, everyone will run towards the exit, chaos will ensue, and a much smaller proportion of the crowd will escape the fire. Put succinctly, in social dilemmas, individual rationality leads to collective irrationality.[xxii]

Social dilemmas have been studied extensively in a number of different fields, including economics, psychology, sociology, and political science. Three representative stories or scenarios are often used to illustrate different types of dilemmas: the prisoner's dilemma, the public good dilemma, and the tragedy of the commons. The prisoner's dilemma is discussed below. The public good dilemma, and associated free-rider problems, were introduced earlier in the context of market failure. The tragedy of the commons involves a shared resource, such as common grazing land, or the population of fish in a common fishing area. In this scenario, each individual has incentive to use as much of the resource as possible while avoiding responsibility for management or maintenance. The result is often collectively irrational neglect and depletion of the shared resource—a resource that, if better managed, would yield significantly more value for everyone.

Social dilemmas are common in developed economies. They are evident in efforts to control pollution, establish technological standards, and deal with environmental issues. An understanding of the incentives created by social dilemmas helps explain the lobbying efforts of "special interest" groups, the behavior of companies involved in format wars, and why social problems, like littering, tax avoidance, and poaching are so persistent. Resolving social dilemmas can often create significant economic value. For example, implementing an effective tax system that minimizes free-riding may make it possible to produce public goods that are many times more valuable than the inputs required to produce them (e.g., a national highway system, public parks, and libraries).

The PCMM assumes that the value buyers and sellers ascribe to a given transaction is independent of the behavior of other market participants. Several types of market failure can be linked to the violation of this assumption (e.g., externalities, public goods, network externalities). A defining characteristic of social dilemmas, in contrast to the PCMM, is that participant behavior is *not* independent. This suggests that the incentives or payoffs to one participant are dependent on the behavior of other participants.[xxiii] Because the assumptions about the nature of social interaction are different in social dilemmas than in the PCMM or in a market failure approach, the incentives and dynamics of a typical prisoner's dilemma are described in greater detail in the following section.

The Prisoner's Dilemma

The prisoner's dilemma gets its name from the original backstory created by Albert Tucker and Melvin Dresher, two scientists at RAND Corporation in Santa Monica, California, who developed the dilemma in 1950 and used it in an informal experiment.[xxiv] In the original scenario, a law enforcement representative offers two prisoners the opportunity to provide evidence against each other in exchange for leniency. They are each informed that if both choose to provide evidence, then the offer of leniency will be retracted and each will receive a relatively long sentence. On the other hand, if neither informs on the other, then the officer admits that each is likely to receive a relatively light sentence. The inducement, explains the officer, is that if one prisoner provides evidence and the other does not, then the cooperating prisoner will be rewarded with a particularly light sentence while the other will be punished with a particularly long sentence. In other words, there are four possible outcomes: a) both prisoners cooperate; b) the first prisoner cooperates, but the second prisoner does not; c) the first prisoner refuses to cooperate, but the second prisoner does; and, d) neither prisoner cooperates. Payoffs for each prisoner for each possible outcome are displayed in Figure 3.1.

In each cell, the prison sentence for Prisoner 1 is displayed in the upper-left and the sentence for Prisoner 2 appears in the bottom-right. The sum of the two prisoners' sentences for each outcome appears in parentheses in the top-left of each cell. For example, the numbers in the top-left cell represent the outcomes for each prisoner if neither prisoner confesses. In this case, each receives a three-year sentence. The bottom-left cell indicates the sentence for

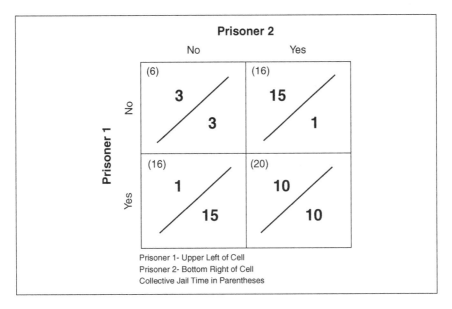

FIGURE 3.1   Prisoner's Dilemma Payoff Matrix

each prisoner if Prisoner 1 confesses (1 year), but Prisoner 2 does not (15 years). The top-right cell is the mirror image of the bottom-left cell: Prisoner 1 refuses to confess (and receives 15 years), while Prisoner 2 confesses (and is rewarded with a 1-year sentence). Finally, in the bottom-right cell, both prisoners confess and each receives a 10-year sentence.

The shaded arrows in Figure 3.2 represent the choices available to Prisoner 1. If he or she believes that Prisoner 2 will refuse to confess, then he or she is left to choose between a three-year sentence and a one-year sentence. This choice is represented by the shaded arrow that extends from the upper-left cell to the upper-right cell. On the other hand, if he or she believes that Prisoner 2 will confess, then he or she is left to choose between a fifteen-year sentence and a ten-year sentence (represented by the shaded arrow extending from the bottom-left cell to the bottom-right cell). Regardless of what Prisoner 2 does, Prisoner 1 is always better off confessing. Similarly, Prisoner 2 faces the same decision set (represented by the outlined arrows). Each prisoner, therefore, is always better off confessing regardless of what the other prisoner does. If each prisoner behaves rationally, each will confess, and each will receive a ten-year sentence. This outcome is represented in the bottom-right cell.

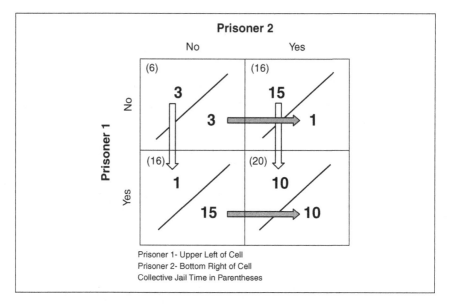

FIGURE 3.2 Prisoner's Dilemma Decision Arrows

Take a moment to examine Figure 3.2. Assuming both prisoners prefer to avoid jail time, the best joint outcome is for neither to confess. This outcome—represented in the top-left cell—yields a total of six years for the two prisoners. In order to realize this joint outcome, however, both prisoners must refuse to confess, thereby forgoing the possibility of being rewarded with a single year in prison, and simultaneously exposing themselves to the risk of being sentenced to fifteen years. In other words, in order to realize the best possible joint outcome, each prisoner is required to act in a manner that is inconsistent with his or her immediate self-interest.

In properly functioning economic markets, individual and collective interests are aligned. In social dilemmas, in contrast, individual interests conflict with collective interests. In Figure 3.2, for example, if both prisoners act in their own self-interest, they will both confess. The result will be a combined total of twenty years in jail—the worst possible joint outcome.

How groups of people, communities and societies resolve social dilemmas is the focus of an extensive and expanding body of research that spans a number of different social science disciplines. Different solutions have focused on the value orientations of participants, participant communication, the role of group identity, reciprocity, social norms, social learning, and different structural changes, including altering the frequency or time horizon of interaction, and changing the payoff structure (or incentives) by introducing additional rewards and sanctions.[xxv] At least two factors are important in the resolution of social dilemmas. First, it is important that participants be made aware of the dilemma, so that they can factor moral, normative, and altruistic considerations into their decision making. Second, it is important that participants believe that other participants will resist the temptation to act in their own self-interest.[xxvi] CSR can play an important role in the resolution of social dilemmas by increasing awareness, enhancing normative constraints on self-interested behavior, and introducing other incentives for cooperative behavior.

VALUE CREATION

This chapter began with a question: As a society, what, exactly, do we want from our economic system?

Both Bowen's list of eleven macroeconomic objectives and Davis and Bomstrom's list of potential areas of social involvement can be succinctly subsumed in this statement: We want our economic system to create value. In this context, value is a subjective attribution of relative worth. We want our economic system to use resources to create products and services that we value more than the resources used to produce them. As Wheeler and colleagues assert, the "creation of value is the central motive force of market economies, and by extension the primary purpose of private enterprise."[xxvii]

The second question that was asked at the beginning of the chapter was this: How do we get there? Stated more formally, assuming that we, as a society, know what we want from our economic system, and assuming that businesses recognize an obligation to contribute to the realization of these objectives, what does CSR suggest about how businesses should behave?

If answered broadly, the answer to this question is fairly straightforward. From a CSR perspective, businesses should be committed to creating economic value, given that that is what society expects from its economic system.

What specifically, should businesses do to create economic value? Should they focus on maximizing profit? Should they focus on other economic, social, or environmental measures? Should businesses act in ways that may not be in their immediate interest, but that have the potential to lead to superior group or collective outcomes? The answer to these questions is this: It depends. It depends on the type of good or service, on the existence of market-supporting social institutions, and on whether or not basic market conditions can be satisfied. It depends on whether or not there are significant externalities, monopolistic or oligopolistic market conditions, network externalities, information problems or other problems with market structure that insulate companies from competitive pressure. And finally, it depends on whether or not there are conflicts between individual and collective interests.

When markets are properly structured and sufficiently competitive, a focus on profit maximization may be the most direct way to contribute to the social good. In the case of market failure, however, an exclusive focus on profits may lead to inefficient, suboptimal, or even catastrophic outcomes, and in these cases, profit measures will be poor indicators of whether or not businesses have created economic value. In the case of social dilemmas, CSR may require businesses to subordinate their individual interests to collective interests in order to avoid the trap of collective irrationality.

Regardless of the context, a commitment to CSR requires a commitment to value creation. The PCMM, market failure, and social dilemmas should be viewed as different frameworks for linking individual behavior to group or system outcomes. CSR requires businesses to know when each is appropriate, and to regulate their efforts to create economic value accordingly.

CHAPTER SUMMARY

Societies expect certain outcomes from their economic systems. Because market participants have an obligation to contribute to outcomes that satisfy societal expectations, these expectations anchor the concept of CSR.

The perfect competition market model (or PCMM) is a good representation of commonly held beliefs about how markets work. It is often used to link business behavior to macroeconomic outcomes. In order for the PCMM to function properly, however, a number of conditions must be met, including a large number of independent buyers and sellers, no participant pricing power, product homogeneity, no barriers to entry or exit, no artificial restraints on prices, and participants must be fully informed. If these conditions are met, the most effective way for businesses to contribute to productive and allocative efficiency, and the maximization of social surplus, may be to seek to maximize profit. This approach to CSR has become known as the Friedman Doctrine.

Although the PCMM reflects a common understanding of economic markets, it is not the only way of connecting business behavior to macroeconomic outcomes. The term "market failure" describes situations in which markets fail to function properly. There are a number of different causes of market failure, including externalities, public goods, monopolies and oligopolies, natural monopolies, network externalities, information problems, and other structural idiosyncrasies. In cases of market failure, profit measures will be poor indicators of whether or not businesses have created economic value, and attempts to maximize profits can lead to inefficient, suboptimal, or even catastrophic outcomes.

Social dilemmas—defined as "interaction situations in which rational individual behavior produces irrational group or collective outcomes"—represent another approach to linking individual behavior and group or system outcomes.[xxviii] In social dilemmas, participant behavior is not independent, and the incentives or payoffs to participants vary based on the behavior of other participants. One of the representative stories or scenarios generally used to illustrate social dilemmas—the prisoner's dilemma—is described in detail in order to illustrate how these dilemmas work. In contrast to properly functioning economic markets, in social dilemmas individual interests conflict with collective interests, and in order to realize the best possible outcome, participants may be required to act in a manner that is inconsistent with their immediate self-interest.

We want our economic system to create value in the sense that we want it to use resources to create products and services that we value more than we value the resources used to produce them. CSR demands that businesses be committed to creating economic value, given that that is what society expects from its economic system. The PCMM, market failure, and social dilemmas should be viewed as different frameworks for linking individual behavior to group or system outcomes. CSR requires businesses to know when each is appropriate, and to regulate their efforts to create economic value accordingly.

REVIEW QUESTIONS

1. What do we, as a society, want from our economic system?

2. Explain why it is difficult to link individual participants' behavior to group or system outcomes.

3. What is the perfect competition market model (PCMM)? Why is it important to a discussion of CSR?

4. What is the Friedman Doctrine? In cases of market failure, or in social dilemmas, would the application of the Friedman Doctrine produce good macroeconomic outcomes? Why or why not? Explain.

5. List and then explain the different causes of market failure.

6. What is a social dilemma? Explain the concept of collective irrationality and why it is important to a discussion of CSR.

7. Explain the prisoner's dilemma. Why is the prisoner's dilemma interesting?

8. From a CSR perspective, why is a focus on value creation important?

ENDNOTES

[i]Bowen, H. R. 1953. *Social responsibilities of the businessman.* New York: Harper & Row, pgs. 8–12.

[ii]Davis, K. and Blomstrom, R. L. 1971. *Business, society, and environment: Social power and social response* (2nd ed.). New York: McGraw-Hill Book Company.

[iii]Smith, A. 1776/1976. *An inquiry into the nature and causes of the wealth of nations.* Chicago: University of Chicago Press.

[iv]Although this quote is frequently attributed to John Maynard Keynes, there is some doubt about whether not this attribution is correct. See http://quoteinvestigator.com/2011/02/23/capitalism-motives/, and also http://www.barrypopik.com/index.php/new_york_city/entry/capitalism_is_the_belief_that_the_wickedest_of_men_will_do_wickedest_things/.

[v]See Schelling, T. C. 1978. *Micromotives and macrobehavior.* New York: W. W. Norton & Company; This concept is closely related to research on social dilemmas. For a good overview, see Kollock, P. 1998. Social dilemmas: The anatomy of cooperation. *Annual Review of Sociology,* 24: 183–214.

[vi]Kuttner, R. 1996. *Everything for sale: The virtues and limits of markets.* New York: Alfred A. Knopf, pg. 3.

[vii]For an accessible, but thorough, discussion of the perfect competition market model, see Chapter 2 of Walters, S. J. K. 1993. *Enterprise, government, and the public.* New York: McGraw-Hill. For a more advanced treatment of the same, see Bator, F. M. 1957. The simple analytics of welfare maximization. *American Economic Review,* 47(1): 22–59, and Bator, F. M. 1958. The anatomy of market failure. *The Quarterly Journal of Economics,* 72(3): 351–379.

[viii]See Walters, S. J. K. 1993. *Enterprise, government, and the public.* New York: McGraw-Hill, Chapter 2.

[ix]See Friedman, M. 1970. The social responsibility of business is to increase its profits. *New York Times Magazine,* September 13.

[x]These paragraphs are excerpted from Friedman, M. 1970. The social responsibility of business is to increase its profits. *New York Times Magazine,* September 13.

[xi]Although Milton Friedman is generally viewed as the most articulate proponent of this brand of CSR criticism, he is not alone. For additional insight into this line of CSR criticism, see Collins, D. 1996. Capitalism and sin. *Business and Society,* 35(1): 42–50; Davis, K. 1973. The case for and against business assumption of social responsibilities. *Academy of Management Journal,* 16(2): 312–322; Frederick, W. C. 1960. The growing concern over business responsibility. *California Management Review,* 2: 54–61; Jones, M. T. 1996. Missing the forest for the trees. *Business and Society,* 35(1): 7–41; Shaffer, B. D. 1977. The social responsibility of business: A dissent. *Business and Society,* 17(2): 11–18.

[xii]Francis M. Bator was one of the first economists to use this term: Bator, F. M. 1958. The anatomy of market failure. *The Quarterly Journal of Economics,* 72(3): 351–379.

[xiii]http://en.wikipedia.org/wiki/Financial_crisis_of_2007–2008.

[xiv]Beal, B. D. 2012. Competitive markets, collective action, and the Big Box Retailer problem. *Journal of Philosophical Economics,* 6(1): 2–29, pg. 12.

[xv]Bator, F. M. 1958. The anatomy of market failure. *The Quarterly Journal of Economics,* 72(3): 351–379, pg. 351.

[xvi]Ayres, I. and Levitt, S. D. 1998. Measuring positive externalities from unobservable victim precaution: An empirical analysis of Lojack. *Quarterly Journal of Economics,* 113(1): 43–77.

[xvii]Nobel Prize lectures are available at http://www.nobelprize.org; Coase's 1991 lecture is available here: http://www.nobelprize.org/nobel_prizes/economics/laureates/1991/coase-lecture.html.

[xviii]Pepall, L., Richards, D. J., and Norman, G. 2005. *Industrial organization: Contemporary theory and practice* (3rd ed.). Mason, OH: South-Western.

[xix]For a good overview of network externalities or network effects, see Arthur, W. B. 1989. Competing technologies, increasing returns, and lock-in by historical events. *The Economic Journal*, 99(394): 116–131; Katz, M. and Shapiro, C. 1985. Network externalities, competition and compatibility. *American Economic Review*, 75(3): 424–440; Katz, M. L. and Shapiro, C. 1986. Technology adoption in the presence of network externalities. *Journal of Political Economy*, 94(4): 822–841; Liebowitz, S. J. and Margolis, S. E. 1994. Network externality: An uncommon tragedy. *Journal of Economic Perspectives*, 8(2): 133–150.

[xx]The classic paper on information problems is Akerlof's The Market for Lemons: Akerlof, G. A. 1970. The market for "lemons": Quality uncertainty and the market mechanism. *Quarterly Journal of Economics*, 84(3): 488–500; Also see Stigler, G. J. 1961. The Economics of Information. *Journal of Political Economy*, 69(3): 213–225.

[xxi]Levitin, A. J. 2008. Priceless? The economic costs of credit card merchant restraints. *UCLA Law Review*, 55(5): 1321–1405.

[xxii]For an overview of social dilemmas, see Dawes, R. M. 1980. Social dilemmas. *Annual Review of Psychology*, 31(1): 169–193; Heckathorn, D. D. 1996. The dynamics and dilemmas of collective action. *American Sociological Review*, 61: 250–277; Kollock, P. 1998. Social dilemmas: The anatomy of cooperation. *Annual Review of Sociology*, 24: 183–214; and Schelling, T. C. 1978. *Micromotives and macrobehavior*. New York: W. W. Norton & Company.

[xxiii]See Dawes, R. M. 1980. Social dilemmas. *Annual Review of Psychology*, 31(1): 169–193; Heckathorn, D. D. 1996. The dynamics and dilemmas of collective action. *American Sociological Review*, 61: 250–277.

[xxiv]Kollock, P. 1998. Social dilemmas: The anatomy of cooperation. *Annual Review of Sociology*, 24: 183–214, pg. 185.

[xxv]For a good overview of different approaches to resolving social dilemmas, see Kollock, P. 1998. Social dilemmas: The anatomy of cooperation. *Annual Review of Sociology*, 24: 183–214.

[xxvi]Dawes, R. M. 1980. Social dilemmas. *Annual Review of Psychology*, 31(1): 169–193.

[xxvii]Wheeler, D., Colbert, B., and Freeman, R. E. 2003. Focusing on value: Reconciling corporate social responsibility, sustainability and a stakeholder approach in a network world. *Journal of General Management*, 28(3): 1–28, pg. 2.

[xxviii]Beal, B. D. 2012. Competitive markets, collective action, and the Big Box Retailer problem. *Journal of Philosophical Economics*, 6(1): 2–29, pg. 12.

4

The CSR Debate

In 2005, in a special section devoted to CSR in the *Economist*, Clive Crook argues that the CSR movement has won the battle of ideas. "In public-relations terms, their victory is total," he laments. "Corporate social responsibility is now an industry in its own right," he continues, "and a flourishing profession as well. . . . But what does it all amount to, really?"[i]

But what does it all amount to, really? That's a good question.

CSR is unique in at least two ways. First, it is a relatively new concept that is in a state of flux. The CSR debate is fluid and the ideas behind it—including, even, what to call it (see Chapter 1)—are still evolving. Although an argument could be made that the core ideas and assumptions have started to solidify, the same cannot be said of many of the practical aspects of implementation.

Second, for you, the reader, CSR is more than an interesting idea or an academic exercise. CSR is a set of ideas and norms about how businesses are linked—or should be linked—to the larger social system in which they are embedded. What CSR means depends on what you—as a consumer, investor, employee, contractor, member of the community, and in other roles—think about how businesses should operate. Because you are a part of the social system in which businesses are embedded, in a very real sense, CSR is what you think it is (and it will be as effective as you make it).

Because CSR is a normative framework, and therefore dependent on the expectations and demands you introduce into your everyday interactions with businesses, it is important to understand the exchange of ideas that has taken place over the last fifty years about its legitimacy and effectiveness.

TYPES OF CSR

Before addressing specific arguments, it is important to recognize that CSR is often used as an "umbrella" term that brings together a number of different approaches or perspectives (see Chapter 1). As one scholar put it, "the term is a brilliant one; it means something, but not always the same thing, to everybody."[ii] Another scholar has asserted that CSR should be viewed as an "identifying brand" but not "a theoretically nor empirically viable construct."[iii]

Figure 4.1 depicts a basic framework for differentiating different kinds of CSR.[iv] In this framework, CSR activities are positioned along two dimensions: exchange type and level orientation.

The first dimension, exchange type, refers to the nature of the underlying resource exchange involved in a particular business activity. As the term suggests, CSR is concerned with *corporate* social responsibility. Although the word "corporate" can be defined as an adjective meaning "united," "combined," or "collective," in this context it should be understood as an adjective derived from the word "corporation." The word "corporate," therefore, serves to limit the scope of CSR to businesses and business activity. In its most basic form, business involves the process of acquiring, through economic exchange, control over certain resources, manipulating those resources, and then exchanging a final product or service for more resources. Resources may be tangible or intangible. Tangible resources can be further categorized as financial, organizational, physical, and/or technological. Examples of intangible resources include human resources, innovative ability, and firm reputation.[v]

By definition, therefore, economic exchange—defined as the transfer of control over resources—is an essential element of business activity. In Figure 4.1, two types of exchanges are represented—resource-seeking exchanges and unilateral exchanges. Resource-seeking exchanges are driven by the possibility of mutual benefit. In these situations, two parties place greater value on the resources controlled by the other, and each party's motivation is clear: To improve its resource position. Capitalist political economy, in general, and the perfect competition market model or PCMM (see Chapter 3), in particular, is based on this kind of voluntary, mutually-beneficial resource exchange.[vi]

On the other hand, there are times when businesses give up control of certain resources without any expectation of reciprocation or resource gain. When a corporation quietly supports a worthwhile community cause, or anonymously donates money (or other resources) to a local charity, it is not engaging in the same kind of exchanges that characterize its core business activities. Charitable giving or philanthropy, therefore, involves what is referred to as the unilateral transfer of resources (see Figure 4.1). Although it is true that other types of resource exchanges can be envisioned—for example, exchanges that are involuntary (e.g., theft) or that occur under duress (e.g., armed robbery)—these kinds of exchanges are generally not part of legitimate business activity.[vii]

The second dimension, level orientation, is a descriptive continuum that describes the degree to which firms intentionally strive to contribute to group or collective outcomes. When a firm is concerned about how its behavior will contribute to (or detract from) the realization of these kinds of outcomes, it exhibits a macro-level orientation. In contrast, when a firm is only concerned about how its behavior will directly impact itself, it is exhibiting a micro-level orientation. Put another way, level orientation describes the degree to which a firm is willing to "outsource" to the market concern for collective or socioeconomic outcomes. If a firm focuses entirely on maximizing shareholder return, trusting entirely in the ability of the market mechanism to insure that its behavior contributes to societal objectives—then the firm is exhibiting a micro-level orientation. On the other hand, if a firm conscientiously strives to assess, on an ongoing basis, the link between its actions and desired socioeconomic outcomes, and then regulates its behavior in order to contribute to the realization of these outcomes, it is exhibiting a macro-level orientation.

Traditional market-based business activity is, by definition, resource seeking, and is characterized by a micro-level orientation. It is represented in Figure 4.1 by the circle labeled "traditional business." In addition to traditional business activity, three types of CSR are represented. First, there is strategic CSR, also referred to as the business case for CSR, or enlightened self-interest. This is represented by a larger or expanded circle around traditional business activity. Strategic CSR involves finding new or innovative approaches to balancing the interests of stakeholders in ways that enhance firm profitability. Because these efforts are directly linked to firm performance, they remain in the micro-level domain of the level orientation continuum. Given that associated resource exchanges are driven by mutual-benefit, these activities continue to fall within the resource-seeking domain of the exchange type continuum. Nevertheless, strategic CSR reflects a significant level of organizational awareness and sensitivity to CSR principles. In this respect, strategic CSR should be conceptualized as a healthy expansion of the domain of traditional business activity.

When a firm intentionally engages in resource exchanges that involve the unilateral transfer of resources, and these exchanges are driven primarily by concerns about the exchange itself or the exchange partner (e.g., the specific use of the resources, or the characteristics of the recipient), then the firm is engaging in philanthropic CSR. Finally, when a firm is primarily concerned with insuring that its business activities contribute to the realization of desired group or collective outcomes, the firm is engaging in systemic CSR.

Different arguments for and against CSR often focus on one type of CSR, often without making this focus explicit. Because strategic, philanthropic, and systemic CSR are different in important respects, this framework simplifies the CSR debate by helping to make sure that advocates and critics are discussing the same CSR behaviors.

ARGUMENTS FOR CSR

From a strategic CSR perspective (see Figure 4.1), one of the primary questions businesses are interested in is this: Are companies that use CSR to broaden their traditional business activities in ways that are generally perceived to be socially responsible more profitable than companies that fail to do so? Stated more simply: Is CSR related to profitability? Specific questions from this perspective might include the following: Are businesses that successfully exploit increasing demand for products made from reclaimed or recycled materials generally more profitable than other companies? Or this: Are companies that allow their employees to telecommute

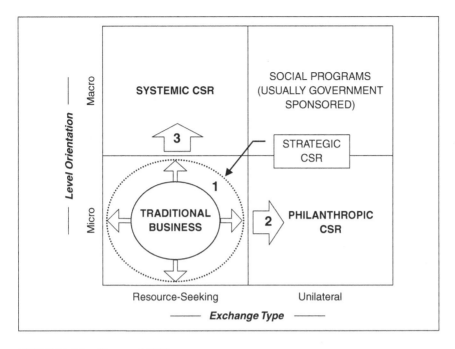

FIGURE 4.1 Types of CSR

in order to reduce motor vehicle emissions more profitable than other companies? Attempts to legitimize or justify CSR by linking it to profit is often referred to as "the business case" for CSR.[viii]

The Business Case for CSR

The business case for CSR rests on the claim that CSR efforts can create significant value for companies. A number of different arguments for how CSR can increase profitability have been put forward. For example, it has been suggested that CSR programs can enhance an organization's legitimacy and reputation, increase its ability to adapt to a changing market place, and make it more likely that the firm will be able to structure synergistic or win-win relationships with its exchange partners.[ix] In addition, several scholars have argued that CSR activity generates a kind of moral capital or insurance that mitigates the negative reactions of stakeholders in situations in which it appears that the firm has failed to act in stakeholder interests.[x]

TABLE 4.I Business Case for CSR

Category	Explanation
Cost & Risk Reduction	Firms can mitigate the costs and risks associated with dissatisfied stakeholders by engaging in appropriate levels of CSR. For example, good governance practices may result in cheaper access to capital, or increased attention to environmental concerns may result in fewer lawsuits.
Profit Maximization & Competitive Advantage	Responsiveness to stakeholder demands may lead to significant market opportunites and the development of valuable capabilities. For example, firms that respond effectively to demands that the needs of consumers in less-developed countries be addressed may be better positioned to take advantage of future opportunities in those countries, or firms that develop the ability to adapt and respond effectively to current stakeholder demands may be better able to deal with future uncertainty and change.
Reputation & Legitimacy	Firms that engage in CSR may be given more operational flexibility (or "license to operate") and may benefit from enhanced goodwill or reputation that may serve as a potentially valuable form of differentiation.
Synergistic Value Creation	C5R efforts may allow companies to identify ways of creating joint value as a part of a network or social system by making it possible for individual companies to transcend a focus on individual interests.

Arguments linking CSR to firm profitability can be grouped into four broad categories based on how CSR is assumed to create value for the firm. These categories are: cost and risk reduction, profit maximization and competitive advantage, reputation and legitimacy, and synergistic value creation.[xi] These categories are summarized in Table 4.1.

CSR and Business Performance

Research on the link between CSR and various measures of business performance, including stock price and various profitability measures, is inconclusive.[xii] CSR activities do not appear to contribute in a systematic way to enhanced performance. This research does suggest, however, that it is possible for businesses to engage in CSR without it negatively impacting profitability.[xiii]

There are a number of problems with the way the relationship between CSR and profitability has been approached. In many cases, the question of what should qualify as CSR hasn't been adequately addressed. For example, as illustrated in Figure 4.1, there are significant differences between strategic, philanthropic, and systemic CSR. In the case of systemic CSR, for example, only efforts that contribute to desired group or macroeconomic outcomes should be considered CSR. From this perspective, identifying CSR efforts is difficult because the link between individual actions and collective outcomes is often complex, counterintuitive, and context dependent. Furthermore, in the case of systemic CSR, particularly in the case of social dilemmas, attempting to link CSR to the performance of individual businesses misses the point—in these situations, CSR should be associated with superior group or collective outcomes, not individual outcomes.

In the case of strategic CSR, the question of what behavior should qualify is equally problematic. In research from this perspective, it often appears that CSR is defined as any effort by businesses that is perceived to be compassionate, socially progressive, or to address the needs of marginalized stakeholders. In addition, because these efforts are motivated by the potential for profit, it is often difficult to distinguish CSR from traditional business activities, or to explain why certain activities are considered CSR and others are not. In the case of philanthropic CSR, although it may be relatively easy to measure, it is often difficult to disentangle from traditional marketing efforts or other self-interested attempts to enhance organizational legitimacy or reputation. These concerns, together with a number of other theoretical and methodological issues,[xiv] suggest that research conclusions regarding the link between CSR and firm performance should be viewed skeptically.

Other Arguments for CSR

More general arguments for the importance of CSR appeal to enlightened self-interest and the desire to avoid societal interference. From an enlightened self-interest perspective, CSR activities contribute to a healthy society, and a healthy society is a better environment for business. From the perspective of avoiding outside interference, if businesses want to be left alone to pursue their interests, they should refrain from engaging in harmful behavior that may require outside intervention to ameliorate.[xv]

A fairly thorough list of reasons for businesses to engage in CSR, published by Keith Davis in 1973, includes the following: long-run self-interest, public image, long-run viability of business as an institution, avoidance of government regulation, compliance with sociocultural norms, stockholder interests, the failure of other institutions to address difficult social problems, possession of the resources, capabilities, and innovative capacity to address difficult social problems, the potential to discover unrecognized business opportunities, and finally, it may be cheaper for business to preventively address social problems now than wait for crises to develop.[xvi]

Michael E. Porter, in a recent article in the *Harvard Business Review,* argues that there are four prevailing justifications for CSR: moral obligation, sustainability (i.e., environmental and community stewardship), license to operate (i.e., the Iron Law of Responsibility), and reputation.[xvii] The first justification, moral obligation, is the argument that firms have a duty, by virtue of their participation in civil society, to "do the right thing." Sustainability arguments focus primarily on environmental stewardship and encourage firms to consider the costs, not only to current stakeholders, but also to future generations, of doing harm to the natural environment. License to operate arguments recognize that firms must have the support of different stakeholders in order to operate. Finally, reputation is often used to justify CSR initiatives, given the potential for these initiatives to contribute to valuable intangible assets, such as morale, image, and brand.

Davis's suggestion that businesses engage in CSR in order to address difficult social problems, such as poverty, unemployment, or income disparity, is generally addressed by contributing resources to philanthropic organizations. For example, research conducted by The Committee Encouraging Philanthropy, one of the largest international business organizations dedicated to promoting corporate philanthropy, reported that the majority of corporate giving in 2012 was directed towards community and economic development, education, and health and social services.[xviii] This kind of giving would be classified as philanthropic CSR in Figure 3.1. Several of the other more general arguments (e.g., long-run self-interest, stockholders' interests, reputation) belong in the strategic CSR category. Arguments that deal directly with collective or socioeconomic outcomes (e.g., contributing to a healthy society, contributing to positive collective outcomes in order to avoid external regulation, preserving business as an institution) are systemic in nature, and are therefore appropriately classified as systemic CSR.

Although the categories in Figure 4.1 are fairly broad, and in some cases, different rationales may not fit neatly into just one category, the framework nevertheless provides a useful structure for organizing different approaches to justify CSR activity.

ARGUMENTS AGAINST CSR

In 1958, Theodore Levitt published an article in the *Harvard Business Review* entitled "The Dangers of Social Responsibility."[xix] In this article, Levitt argued against, among other things, the "new feudalism" represented by attempts to saddle businesses with additional social responsibilities. According to Levitt, "we are against the all-embracing welfare state not because we are against welfare but because we are against centralized power and the harsh social discipline it so ineluctably produces. We do not want a pervasive welfare state in government, and we do not want it in unions. And for the same reasons we should not want it in corporations."[xx] Levitt was convinced that "the power which the corporation gains as a sort of commercial demichurch it will lose as an agency of profit-motive capitalism. Indeed, as the profit motive becomes increasingly sublimated, capitalism will become only a shadow—the torpid remains of the creative dynamism which was and might have been."[xxi] In Levitt's view, it is critical to maintain a clear dividing line between business and government. The domain of business is to maximize profit; establishing the rules of the game, so to speak, and taking care of the general welfare, is the domain of government.

More nuanced arguments against CSR include the following:
a) The function of business is economic in nature and the best way

for firms to fulfill that function is to maximize profits, b) The additional costs of shouldering social responsibilities will drive marginal firms out of business, c) Businesses do not have the appropriate skill sets or the right motivation to effectively address social issues, d) Involvement in social issues may distract firms from their core economic functions, e) Business, considered as an institution, has enough power; allowing business to exercise its influence in social arenas puts at risk the existing pluralistic balance between different institutions and could, therefore, threaten free society, f) Business managers are not elected and would therefore have no direct accountability to society, and, g) There is considerable resistance from different groups to the involvement of businesses in social issues.[xxii]

Recently, Aneel Karnani argued in a special report in the *Wall Street Journal* that CSR is "an illusion, and a potentially dangerous one."[xxiii] In this report, Karnani argues that in cases in which the private pursuit of profit is likely to enhance the general welfare, the concept of CSR isn't needed and is irrelevant. In properly functioning competitive markets, this is likely to be the case. In circumstances in which the pursuit of profit is unlikely to enhance the social welfare, CSR will be ineffective, given that CSR requires businesses to act in ways that are not in their immediate interests. The real danger is not that CSR will be ineffective; it's that CSR may give society a false sense of security and work to prevent the implementation of effective regulation. Similar arguments are made in greater detail in a recent book by David Vogel entitled *The Market for Virtue: The Potential and Limits of Corporate Social Responsibility.*[xxiv]

The following is an excerpt from the special report on CSR referenced above. As you read it, think of how you would defend CSR against these arguments if you were called upon to do so.

Large companies now routinely claim that they aren't in business just for the profits, that they're also intent on serving some larger social purpose. They trumpet their efforts to produce healthier foods or more fuel-efficient vehicles, conserve energy and other resources in their operations, or otherwise make the world a better place. Influential institutions like the Academy of Management and the United Nations, among many others, encourage companies to pursue such strategies. It's not surprising that this idea has won over so many people—it's a very appealing proposition. You can have your cake and eat it too!

But it's an illusion, and a potentially dangerous one.

Very simply, in cases where private profits and public interests are aligned, the idea of corporate social responsibility is irrelevant: Companies that simply do everything they can to boost profits will end up increasing social welfare. In circumstances in which profits and social welfare are in direct opposition, an appeal to corporate social responsibility will almost always be ineffective, because executives are unlikely to act voluntarily in the public interest and against shareholder interests.

Irrelevant or ineffective, take your pick. But it's worse than that. The danger is that a focus on social responsibility will delay or discourage more-effective measures to enhance social welfare in those cases where profits and the public good are at odds. As society looks to companies to address these problems, the real solutions may be ignored.

. . . .

The ultimate solution is government regulation. Its greatest appeal is that it is binding. Government has the power to enforce regulation. No need to rely on anyone's best intentions.[xxv]

Implicit in Karnani's argument is the notion that CSR, when it is practiced, is generally a fairly superficial effort by firms to pacify different stakeholders, rather than a substantive self-regulatory commitment. In cases where the profit motive is at odds with the public good, in Karnani's view, strong and effective government regulation is required, not an appeal to the better nature of the business community. This criticism suggests that CSR is a distinct or separate responsibility that can be considered independently of economic imperatives. This is apparent, for example, in criticisms that identify CSR as a distraction from "core" activities, and in assertions that businesses don't have the right skill sets or would not be sufficiently accountable if involved in addressing social problems.

Much of this criticism becomes less relevant when CSR is defined in systemic terms. From a systemic perspective, CSR cannot be considered apart from a firm's "core" activities because it plays a critical role in determining what those activities should be and how they should be carried out. In many cases, the most effective rebuttal to CSR critics is the argument that CSR, properly implemented, has the potential to increase the efficiency of economic markets, reduce the need for centralized regulation, and, in the case of market failure, serve as a framework for resolving social dilemmas, thereby decreasing the likelihood of rational irrationality. In other words, CSR has the potential to improve the way our economic system works.

Karnani and others that claim that CSR will be ineffective in changing corporate behavior underestimate the power of social norms. By changing the expectations of customers and other key stakeholders, CSR has the potential to change the incentives faced by corporate decision-makers. The effectiveness of CSR as a normative framework does not depend on firms voluntarily agreeing to act against their self-interest—it depends on the power of social norms to alter the incentives faced by corporations so that it is in their best interest to comply.

CHAPTER SUMMARY

CSR is unique because it is still in the process of being defined and because, as a normative concept, its existence depends on what you—and others—think about it.

It is important to differentiate between different kinds of CSR. Positioning different CSR activities along two dimensions—exchange type and level orientation—yields three different types of CSR: strategic, philanthropic, and systemic. Attempts to legitimize or justify CSR by linking it to firm profitability—sometimes referred to as the business case for CSR—often do so from a strategic CSR perspective. These arguments can be grouped into four categories based on how CSR is assumed to create value for the firm: cost and risk reduction, profit maximization and competitive advantage, reputation and legitimacy, and synergistic value creation. Research on the link between CSR and firm performance is inconclusive.

Because of problems with the way this research has been conducted, conclusions should be viewed skeptically.

Arguments for CSR include an appeal to enlightened self-interest and the desire to avoid societal interference. It has also been argued that businesses should engage in CSR to promote the long-run viability of business as an institution, to comply with societal norms and expectations, and because businesses possess the required resources, capabilities, and innovative capacity to address difficult social problems, among others. Michael E. Porter argues that there are four prevailing justifications for CSR: moral obligation, sustainability (i.e., environmental and community stewardship), license to operate, and reputation.

Arguments against CSR include the assertion that society should maintain a clear dividing line between business and government, and claims that businesses do not have the right skill sets or the right motivation to address social issues, CSR efforts may distract firms from their core economic functions, and that allowing businesses to address social problems may upset the pluralistic balance between different societal institutions. One critic recently claimed that CSR will be ineffective in convincing businesses to act against their own interests, and is therefore dangerous, given that a focus on CSR may undermine societal commitment to effective regulation.

Much of this criticism becomes less relevant when CSR is defined in systemic terms. The most effective rebuttal to CSR critics is often the argument that CSR, properly implemented, has the potential to increase the efficiency of economic markets, reduce the need for centralized regulation, and, in the case of market failure, serve as a framework for resolving social dilemmas, thereby decreasing the likelihood of collective irrationality.

REVIEW QUESTIONS

1. How is CSR different from other business concepts? How are you involved?

2. Explain the difference between strategic, philanthropic, and systemic CSR. Why is it important to distinguish between these different types of CSR?

3. What are four categories of arguments often used to make the business case for CSR?

4. Is there a link between CSR and business profitability? What challenges have researchers looking for this link had to confront? Explain.

5. Briefly summarize at least three arguments for CSR.

6. Briefly summarize at least three arguments against CSR.

7. What do you think about CSR? Why?

ENDNOTES

[i]Crook, C. 2005. The good company. *Economist,* 374(8410): Special Section, 3–4, pg. 3.

[ii]Votaw, D. 1972. Genius becomes rare: A comment on the doctrine of social responsibility, pt. I. *California Management Review,* XV(2): 25–31, pg. 25.

[iii]This quote refers specifically to corporate social performance (CSP), a type of CSR: Rowley, T. J. and Berman, S. L. 2000. A brand new brand of corporate social performance. *Business & Society,* 39(4): 397–418.

[iv]This framework, the associated figure, and the associated discussion are adapted from an unpublished research paper by the author and a colleague: Beal, B. D. and Damoiseau, Y. 2007. Corporate social responsibility: Definition and the micro-to-macro problem. Tyler, TX: The University of Tyler at Texas.

[v]For a discussion of resources in the context of strategic management, see Hill, C. W. L. and Jones, G. R. 2010. *Strategic management: An integrated approach* (9th ed.). Mason, OH: South-Western Cengage Learning; Barney, J. B., and Hesterley, W. S. 2010. *Strategic management and competitive advantage: Concepts* (3rd ed.). Upper Saddle River, NJ: Pearson Prentice Hall; Hitt, M. A., Ireland, R. D., and Hoskisson, R. E. 2009. *Strategic management concepts: Competitiveness and globalization* (8th ed.). Mason, OH: South-Western Cengage Learning; Hall, R. 1992. The strategic analysis of intangible resources. *Strategic Management Journal,* 13(2): 135–144.

[vi]Jones, M. T. 1996. Missing the forest for the trees. *Business and Society,* 35(1): 7–41; Walters, S. J. K. 1993. *Enterprise, government, and the public.* New York: McGraw-Hill.

[vii]For a discussion of the ways in which control over resources may be transferred or exchanged, see Coleman, J. 1990. *Foundations of Social Theory.* Cambridge, MA: Harvard University Press.

[viii]For interesting overview of the business case for CSR, see Kurucz, E. C., Colbert, B. A., and Wheeler, D. 2008. The business case for corporate social responsibility. In A. Crane, A. McWilliams, D. Matten, J. Moon, and D. Siegel (Eds.), *The Oxford handbook of corporate social responsibility:* 83–112. Oxford: Oxford University Press; Also see Aupperle, K. E., Carroll, A. B., and Hatfield, J. D. 1985. An empirical examination of the relationship between corporate social responsibility and profitability.

Academy of Management Journal, 28(2): 446–463; Burke, L. and Logsdon, J. M. 1996. How corporate social responsibility pays off. *Long Range Planning,* 29(August): 495–502; Griffin, J. J. and Mahon, J. F. 1997. The corporate social performance and corporate financial performance debate: Twenty-five years of incomparable research. *Business & Society,* 36(1): 5–31; Orlitzky, M. 2008. Corporate social performance and financial performance: A research synthesis. In A. Crane, A. McWilliams, D. Matten, J. Moon, and D. Siegel (Eds.), *The Oxford handbook of corporate social responsibility:* 113–134. Oxford: Oxford University Press; Schreck, P. 2011. Reviewing the business case for corporate social responsibility: New evidence and analysis. *Journal of Business Ethics,* 103(2): 167–188; Waddock, S. A. and Graves, S. B. 1997. The corporate social performance-financial performance link. *Strategic Management Journal,* 18(4): 303–319.

[ix]For a recent summary of the potential benefits of CSR, see Sprinkle, G. B. and Maines, L. A. 2010. The benefits and costs of corporate social responsibility, *Business Horizons,* Vol. 53: 445–453.

[x]See, for example, Godfrey, P. C., Merrill, C. B., and Hansen, J. M. 2009. The relationship between corporate social responsibility and shareholder value: An empirical test of the risk management hypothesis. *Strategic Management Journal,* 30(4): 425–445.

[xi]These categories are taken from Kurucz, E. C., Colbert, B. A., and Wheeler, D. 2008. The business case for corporate social responsibility. In A. Crane, A. McWilliams, D. Matten, J. Moon, and D. Siegel (Eds.), *The Oxford handbook of corporate social responsibility:* 83–112. Oxford: Oxford University Press.

[xii]For a recent study addressing the link between CSR and performance, see Schreck, P. 2011. Reviewing the business case for corporate social responsibility: New evidence and analysis. *Journal of Business Ethics,* 103(2): 167–188.

[xiii]A recent study of the relationship between CSR and profitability emphasizes this point: Schreck, P. 2011. Reviewing the business case for corporate social responsibility: New evidence and analysis. *Journal of Business Ethics,* 103(2): 167–188.

[xiv]For a good introduction to the problems with research on CSR and performance, see Ullmann, A. A. 1985. Data in search of a theory: A critical examination of the relationships among social performance, social disclosure, and economic performance of U.S. firms. *Academy of Management Review,* 10(3): 540–557, and Rowley, T. J. and Berman, S. L. 2000. A brand new brand of corporate social performance. *Business & Society,* 39(4): 397–418.

[xv]For a summary of these arguments, see Mintzberg, H. 1983. The case for corporate social responsibility. *Journal of Business Strategy,* 4(2): 3–15.

[xvi]Davis, K. 1973. The case for and against business assumption of social responsibilities. *Academy of Management Journal,* 16(2): 312–322; Also see Davis, K. 1960. Can business afford to ignore social responsibilities? *California Management Review,* 2: 70–76; Davis, K. 1967. Understanding the social responsibility puzzle: What does the businessman owe to society? *Business Horizons,* Winter: 45–50; Davis, K. and Blomstrom, R. L. 1971. *Business, society, and environment: Social power and social response* (2nd ed.). New York: McGraw-Hill Book Company.

[xvii]See Porter, M. E. and Kramer, M. R. 2006. Strategy & society: The link between competitive advantage and corporate social responsibility. *Harvard Business Review,* 84(12): 78–92.

[xviii]See http://www.corporatephilanthropy.org/research.html.

[xix]Levitt, T. 1958. The dangers of social responsibility. *Harvard Business Review,* 36(5): 41–50.

[xx]Levitt, T. 1958. The dangers of social responsibility. *Harvard Business Review,* 36(5): 41–50, pg. 44.

[xxi]Levitt, T. 1958. The dangers of social responsibility. *Harvard Business Review,* 36(5): 41–50, pg. 46.

[xxii]This list is drawn primarily from Davis, K. 1973. The case for and against business assumption of social responsibilities. *Academy of Management Journal,* 16(2): 312–322; Also see Mintzberg, H. 1983. The case for corporate social responsibility. *Journal of Business Strategy,* 4(2): 3–15.

[xxiii]See Karnani, A. 2010. The case against corporate social responsibility. *Wall Street Journal (Eastern Edition),* 256(45): R1–R4.

[xxiv]Vogel, D. 2005. *The market for virtue: The potential and limits of corporate social responsiblity.* Washington, DC: Brookings Institution Press; also see Vogel, D. J. 2005. Is there a market for virtue? The business case for corporate social responsibility. *California Management Review,* 47(4): 19–45.

[xxv]See Karnani, A. 2010. The case against corporate social responsibility. *Wall Street Journal (Eastern Edition),* 256(45): R1–R4.

5

The Future of CSR

The concept of CSR will continue to evolve, and that makes charting its future difficult. Despite this uncertainty, this chapter highlights two recent developments: the dramatic increase in the last few years of firms issuing social responsibility reports, and the emergence of two new variants of CSR, conscious capitalism, and creating shared value (CSV).

In addition, a number of different ways of conceptualizing CSR are proposed. The first is based on *The Lorax*, a children's book by Dr. Seuss, while the second partners CSR with market-based competitive pressure. Two additional frameworks suggest that CSR has the capacity to exploit the same information advantages inherent in economic markets, and that CSR may be a useful framework for collectively resolving large scale social dilemmas, respectively.

The chapter concludes with a brief comment on the critical role of taken-for-granted assumptions and shared norms to CSR's ongoing evolution and development.

NEW DEVELOPMENTS

CSR Reporting

According to a 2011 survey-based report published by KPMG, one of the "big four" accounting and auditing firms, 95% of the 250 largest global companies issued CSR or sustainability reports.[i] In 2005, this number was approximately 50%.[ii] This dramatic increase in CSR reporting can be at least partially attributed to increased demands for transparency by important stakeholders, including customers, the media, "watchdog" organizations, and in some cases, investors. The expected content and format of non-financial reporting is also becoming increasingly clear. For example, fairly similar reporting guidelines are now being promoted by organizations like Global Reporting Initiative (GRI), the International Organization for Standardization (ISO), AccountAbility, the United Nations Global Compact, and the Organisation for Economic Co-operation and Development (OECD).[iii] GRI's G3.1 reporting standards were issues in 2011 and their G4 guidelines were scheduled for release in May of 2013.

In addition to these factors, businesses have begun to see the value of CSR reporting, particularly with respect to company image and the ability of the organization to productively communicate with diverse stakeholders. A number of developments have also made reporting easier, including the proliferation of accounting and auditing firms, consultants, and other third parties that offer CSR- and sustainability-related services. Finally, information technology has made it easier for firms to gather and disclose required data.[iv]

As reporting guidelines and stakeholder expectations solidify, pressure on companies to gather and disclose CSR and sustainability data will continue to increase.

Conscious Capitalism

At least two new variants of CSR deserve mention. The first, referred to as conscious capitalism, is associated with John Mackey, the co-founder and co-CEO of Whole Foods Market, a $11.69 billion (FY 2012) Fortune 500 company. In 2005, Mackey took part in a debate on corporate social responsibility with Milton Friedman and T. J. Rodgers, the founder and CEO of Cypress Semiconductor. This debate was published in *Reason*, a libertarian monthly magazine published by the Reason Foundation.[v] Here is a short excerpt:

In 1970 Milton Friedman wrote that "there is one and only one social responsibility of business—to use its resources and engage in activities designed to increase its profits so long as it stays within the rules of the game, which is to say, engages in open and free competition without deception or fraud." . . . I strongly disagree. I'm a businessman and a free market libertarian, but I believe that the enlightened corporation should try to create value for all of its constituencies. . . . The business model that Whole Foods has embraced could represent a new form of capitalism, one that more consciously works for the common good instead of depending solely on the "invisible hand" to generate positive results for society. The "brand" of capitalism is in terrible shape throughout the world, and corporations are widely seen as selfish, greedy, and uncaring. This is both unfortunate and unnecessary, and could be changed if businesses and economists widely adopted the business model that I have outlined here.

Subsequent to this debate, Mackey began referring to the "new form of capitalism," mentioned in the second-to-last paragraph, as "conscious capitalism." In 2009, he published a controversial op-ed piece in the *Wall Street Journal* entitled "The Whole Foods Alternative to ObamaCare" in which he criticized the proposed Affordable Healthcare Act and outlined a number of alternative reforms more consistent with a libertarian political philosophy. This editorial generated significant media attention and gave Mackey a platform to promote his views of capitalism. He trademarked the term "conscious capitalism" and founded Conscious Capitalism, Inc., an organization dedicated to promoting his views.

Conscious capitalism has four core principles: a higher purpose, a stakeholder orientation, conscious leadership, and a conscious culture. In conscious capitalism, profit maximization is not the overriding objective or purpose of the firm. The most important requirement "for the creation of the highest levels of trust and performance" is to focus on a larger sense of purpose: "Why does the business exist? What is it trying to accomplish? What core values will inspire the enterprise and create greater trust and commitment from all of its stakeholders?"[vi] Great businesses will have great purposes, and Mackey links these purposes to the timeless ideals of the good, the true, the beautiful, and the heroic.

In conscious capitalism, six major stakeholders are recognized (customers, employees, suppliers, investors, society, and the environment), and the challenge of leadership is to create value for these stakeholders in harmonious and synergistic ways. Conscious leadership will create a conscious culture in which there is a commitment "to creating a workplace that reflects a community of people who are flourishing and self-actualizing."[vii]

Although Mackey has argued that conscious capitalism is distinct from other forms of CSR, its core principles are reflected to varying degrees in different CSR formulations and approaches. Although conscious capitalism has a more New Age look and feel, it is part of the CSR (or sustainability) family.[viii]

Creating Shared Value

The second new variant of CSR that deserves mention is Michael E. Porter's concept of creating shared value (CSV). Porter leads the Institute for Strategy and Competitiveness at the Harvard Business School; two of his books, *Competitive Strategy: Techniques for Analyzing Industries and Competitors* and *Competitive Advantage: Creating and Sustaining Superior Performance*, published in 1980 and 1985, respectively, are generally recognized as foundational texts in the field of strategic management.

In 2006, with co-author Mark R. Kramer, Porter published an article in the *Harvard Business Review* examining the link between competitive advantage and CSR.[ix] Porter and Kramer suggest that firms should sort social issues into three categories: generic social issues, value chain social impacts, and social dimensions of competitive context. Generic social issues, although important in a general sense, are not directly affected by a firm's activities, and are not likely to impact the firm's long term competitiveness. Value chain social impacts, however, are directly related to a firm's operations, and the social dimensions of competitive context are likely to impact a firm's competitiveness. Once issues are sorted into these categories, firms can begin to develop an explicit corporate social agenda. The first level of involvement—responsive CSR—requires businesses to exhibit good corporate citizenship by working to mitigate any adverse affects of business activities. Strategic CSR goes beyond responsive CSR by requiring firms to focus on a small number of business initiatives that will yield both significant business and social benefits. Strategic CSR requires companies to skillfully manage societal linkages and intentionally incorporate social dimensions into their business model and value proposition. Porter and Kramer's 2006 article concludes with this statement:

> Corporations are not responsible for all the world's problems, nor do they have the resources to solve them all. Each company can identify the particular set of societal problems that it is best equipped to help resolve and from which it can gain the greatest competitive benefit. Addressing social issues by creating shared value will lead to self-sustaining solutions that do not depend on private or government subsidies. When a well-run business applies its vast resources, expertise, and management talent to problems that it understands and in which it has a stake, it can have a greater impact on social good than any other institution or philanthropic organization.[x]

In 2011, with the same co-author, Porter published a second article in the *Harvard Business Review* entitled "Creating Shared Value: How to Reinvent Capitalism—and Unleash a Wave of Innovation and Growth."[xi] In this article, Porter and Kramer suggest that firms can simultaneously create economic and social value in three ways: by creating new products and restructuring existing markets, by increasing productivity in their own value chains, and by working to establish supportive industry clusters.

In Porter and Kramer's CSV framework, not all profit is equal. Profit that is associated with activities that contribute to the social good "represent a higher form of capitalism."[xii] The authors conclude with this:

> Shared value focuses companies on the right kind of profits— profits that create societal benefits rather than diminish them. . . . The moment for an expanded view of value creation has come. . . . Creating shared value represents a broader conception of Adam Smith's invisible hand. It opens the doors of the

pin factory to a wider set of influences. It is not philanthropy but self-interested behavior to create economic value by creating societal value. If all companies individually pursued shared value connected to their particular businesses, society's overall interests would be served. And companies would acquire legitimacy in the eyes of the communities in which they operated, which would allow democracy to work as governments set policies that fostered and supported business. Survival of the fittest would still prevail, but market competition would benefit society in ways we have lost.

As in the case of conscious capitalism, despite claims of uniqueness, CSV's primary components are present in existing CSR approaches and frameworks. Porter and Kramer's emphasis on the link between firm activities and societal value, and their suggestion that firms work to establish supportive industry clusters, for example, echo early work by CSR scholars that emphasizes that "social responsibility is first and foremost a systemic concept."[xiii]

Porter and Kramer also argue that businesses should be aware of the link between their activities and different socioeconomic outcomes, and that there may be times when cooperative or collective efforts are likely to yield more value than traditional profit-maximizing approaches. In this respect, CSV can be viewed as a cooperative approach to the provision of public goods and the resolution of related social dilemmas. Although Porter and Kramer's approach may be fairly radical in certain business circles, as is the case with other aspects of the CSV, similar concepts and arguments have been part of the CSR dialogue since at least the 1950s. Like conscious capitalism, CSV belongs in the CSR family, its claims of distinctiveness notwithstanding.

CONCEPTUAL FRAMES

A conceptual frame is a particular approach or way of thinking about an idea or a concept. The following paragraphs are brief descriptions of different conceptual frames for thinking about the nature and function of CSR. These frames are purposefully left open ended. They are intended to be a starting point for further conceptual development and critical thought.

After reading and thinking about these conceptual frames, try to expand them (or come up with one of your own).

Who Speaks for the Trees?

The Lorax, by Dr. Seuss, is a children's book that was first published in 1971. The book is a thinly disguised morality tale about the dangers of environmental exploitation. In the book, the Once-ler decides to begin clear-cutting Truffula trees (an invention of Dr. Seuss) in a pristine valley in order to manufacture "thneeds" (also an invention of Dr. Seuss). When he cuts down the first tree, the Lorax appears from the stump and "speaks for the trees." He warns the Once-ler of the dangers of his actions.

Accurate prices are essential to proper market functioning. In this context, price accuracy refers to whether or not a given price is an accurate reflection of the relative value of the associated item. Think of the Lorax when he "speaks for the trees" as a representation of everything that is "missing" from a given market price. For example, if a firm generates negative spillovers in the process of manufacturing basketballs, and the harm caused by these spillovers is not reflected in the price, then what impact does this have? What does that mean for a Walmart shopper standing in the sporting goods aisle confronted by a choice of three different basketballs manufactured by three different companies, one of which is the company that generates negative spillovers?

Expand this thinking to include other items or sources of value that may not be represented in market prices. For example, is the value of a clean environment to future generations accurately priced into existing goods? What about industries that require complimentary public goods (e.g., the automobile industry and the national highway system)? Should these industries bear some of the cost of the public infrastructure required to use their products? Why or why not?

Imagine having a conversation with the Lorax about what is missing from market prices? What would the Lorax warn you about? Why?

Can CSR be viewed as an attempt to account for value that isn't captured in market prices? Is this an interesting or useful way to view CSR?

A Contingency Model

CSR can be conceptualized as a normative regulatory framework that channels firm behavior in ways that increase the likelihood that a society's economic system will produce desired outcomes. From this perspective, CSR becomes, in situations characterized by the absence of properly functioning economic markets, the non-market equivalent of Adam Smith's invisible hand. In properly functioning markets, competitive pressure creates the incentives that drive firms to behave in ways that lead to broad levels of efficiency and value creation. When this pressure is absent, or in cases where incentives exist for firms to engage in behavior likely to reduce efficiency or undermine the process of value creation, CSR becomes essential.

This suggests that a contingency view of CSR may be useful. From this perspective, the practical significance of CSR depends—or is contingent on—the level of competitive pressure and other constraints that are likely to drive firms towards efficiency and value creation. The stronger the competition, the less need for CSR. On the other hand, the weaker the competition, the greater the need for CSR.

Viewing CSR from this perspective has a number of implications. For example, it may make sense to promote CSR more heavily in industries in which market failure is more likely, or in contexts characterized by social dilemmas.

Efficient Regulation

In the first line of an article "The Use of Knowledge in Society," published in 1954, Friedrich A. Hayek poses an interesting question: "What is the problem we wish to solve when we try to construct a rational economic order?"[xiv] A few paragraphs later, he answers his own query: "It is rather a problem of how to secure the best use of resources known to any of the members of society, for ends whose relative importance only these individuals know. Or, to put it briefly, it is a problem of the utilization of knowledge not given to anyone in its totality."

Hayek's argument is relatively straightforward. If all the relevant information in an economy could be centralized, then the question of a rational economic order could be reduced to a very large (and complex) problem of constrained optimization. In other words, the question of how the economy should be structured to produce an optimal distribution of goods and services could be formulated as a complex equation that could, in theory, be solved. As Hayek points out, however, this is not the question we should be asking. Given information processing limits, and the fact that certain kinds of embedded or tacit knowledge cannot be centralized, the question becomes how to design an economic system that is capable of exploiting embedded knowledge that is distributed through a broad network of individuals. In the remainder of the article, Hayek makes the case that one of the primary advantages of economic markets over other forms of economic organization (e.g., central planning) is the ability to exploit embedded knowledge that is present within the system, but not known by anyone in its totality.

As a conceptual frame, approach the question of regulation in the same way Hayek approaches the question of economic organization. Think of a network of interacting economic agents. Where is the knowledge located necessary to enforce effective regulation? Can this knowledge be easily centralized? For example, if the objective is to prevent negative spillovers in order to improve market functioning, what needs to be known? By whom?

Does regulation need to be "centrally-planned" in order to be effective? What are the challenges and costs associated with attempting to codify and centralize enough information in order to make such regulation effective? On the other hand, can CSR be viewed as a decentralized regulatory framework capable of exploiting embedded knowledge in the same way that Hayek argues that economic markets are capable of doing? If this is the case, then what advantages might CSR, conceptualized as a normative regulatory framework, have over a centralized regulatory approach?[xv]

Panoptic Prisoner's Dilemmas

The word "panoptic" is derived from "pan," which means "with respect to everything, or fully," and "optos," meaning visible.

Panoptic prisoner's dilemmas (or Panoptic PDs) refer to economy-wide social dilemmas or "traps" that work in the same way as the two-person dilemma outlined in Chapter 3. Think about the two prisoners in the prisoner's dilemma. Imagine that you know nothing about their preferences or the internal incentive structure of the situation, but that you are able to observe their behavior. If both prisoners were to confess, and therefore jointly elect to spend twenty years in jail, would you conclude that they must prefer jail time to freedom? Given that they could have jointly elected to spend six years in jail instead of twenty (see Figure 2.1), wouldn't this conclusion be justified? Why not?

Does the same thing happen in the larger economy? Is it possible that in certain cases we, as market participants, become trapped in a suboptimal quadrant of a prisoner's dilemma payoff matrix? Is it possible that certain macroeconomic outcomes are, in reality, examples of collective irrationality?

Here's an example. Assume that it is cheaper for organizations to require existing employees to work additional hours rather than to hire and train additional employees. Furthermore, assume that in order to induce reluctant employees to work longer hours, firms offer to reward those that do so by promising good evaluations, pay raises, and promotions. These rewards, however, are contingent on employees distinguishing themselves. If all employees put in additional time, then there is no basis for differentiating between employees and no rewards are given. In this case, although employees prefer to work fewer hours, the best outcome for each individual employee is to work additional hours when other employees refuse to do so, given that they will then be rewarded for it.

Does this situation mirror the setup of the prisoner's dilemma in Chapter 3? In this situation, if you were to observe a group of employees working 60 hours a week, could you conclude that these individuals prefer work over leisure time with friends or family? Why or why not?

Might the existence of Panoptic PD explain overtime rules and legal constraints, in a number of countries, on the number of hours an employee is allowed to work per week? Can Panoptic PDs be resolved through legislative or legal means? Why or why not? Can you identify other macroeconomic outcomes that might be examples of Panoptic PDs or collective irrationality?

Can CSR be viewed as a framework for identifying and resolving these kinds of dilemmas? In particular, what aspects of CSR might be useful in this respect?

IT'S UP TO YOU

In the previous chapter, it was argued that CSR is unique in the sense that it is a set of ideas and norms about the relationship between business and society that only exist to the extent that you, the reader, believe that they exist. In other words, CSR is only real to the degree that it is reflected in your expectations and actions. If managers and key stakeholders expect firms to focus on the larger challenge of creating economic value in situations in which a narrow focus on profit is unlikely to contribute to the social good, then firms will do so. Firms will do so because the cost of failing to live up to social expectations will make the pursuit of narrow interests an unattractive option. The power of CSR does not lie in its ability to cajole firms into behaving in ways that are counter to their interests; the power of CSR lies in its ability to alter the incentives confronted by organizations so that it no longer makes sense to pursue courses of action that detract from the public good.

As argued in the preface, CSR is not about obligating firms to go against their interest in order to contribute to economic and social outcomes that society demands, it's about establishing and perpetuating social norms that create incentives that point firms in the right direction. CSR, properly implemented, will make economic markets more transparent, efficient, and effective in serving societal interests.[xvi]

CHAPTER SUMMARY

One of the most pronounced trends in CSR in the last few years is the dramatic increase in social responsibility reporting. For example, according to a recent report by KPMG, in 2011, 95% of the 250 largest global companies issued CSR or sustainability reports.

At least two new variants of CSR have emerged. The first, called conscious capitalism, is associated with John Mackey, the co-founder and co-CEO of Whole Foods Market. In conscious capitalism, six major stakeholders are recognized (customers, employees, suppliers, investors, society, and the environment), and the challenge of leadership is to create value for all stakeholders in harmonious and synergistic ways.

The second CSR variant, championed by Michael E. Porter, is referred to as creating shared value (CSV). From a CSV perspective, firms can simultaneously create economic and social value in three ways: by creating new products and restructuring existing markets, by increasing productivity in their own value chains, and by working to establish supportive industry clusters. Not all profit is equal: profit that is associated with activities that contribute to the social good "represent a higher form of capitalism."[xvii]

Different conceptual frames can be useful for thinking about the nature and function of CSR. For example, CSR can be viewed as a mechanism for making sure that all relevant costs are reflected in the price of a given product or service (and an analogy can be drawn between this function and the Lorax, a character in the Dr. Seuss book, *The Lorax,* who "speaks for the trees"). CSR can also be conceptualized as a normative regulatory framework that serves the same function as competitive pressure, a form of efficient regulation that is able to exploit local or embedded knowledge, and as a framework for collectively resolving broad social dilemmas or situations involving collective irrationality.

The power of CSR lies in its ability to alter the incentives faced by organizations. CSR, properly implemented, will make economic markets more transparent, efficient, and effective in serving societal interests.

REVIEW QUESTIONS

1. What is conscious capitalism? What is creating shared value?

2. What does the Lorax—who speaks for the trees—have to do with CSR?

3. What social purpose does competitive pressure play in properly functioning economic markets? Can CSR play a similar role in situations in which competitive pressure isn't sufficient?

4. What does Hayek's view of the role of knowledge in markets have to do with CSR? Can CSR be viewed as efficient regulation? Explain.

5. Is it possible that certain macroeconomic outcomes are an example of collective irrationality? Can CSR be useful in addressing these outcomes? Explain.

ENDNOTES

[i]KPMG. 2011. International survey of corporate responsibility reporting 2011. Amsterdam: KPMG; Also see previous reports issued in 2002, 2005, and 2008.

[ii]KPMG. 2008. International survey of corporate responsibility reporting 2008. Amsterdam: KPMG; Also see Fifka, M. S. and Drabble, M. 2012. Focus and standardization of sustainability reporting—A comparative study of the United Kingdom and Finland. *Business Strategy and the Environment*, 21(7): 455–474; Fifka, M. S. 2013. Corporate responsibility reporting and its determinants in comparative perspective—A review of the empirical literature and a meta-analysis. *Business Strategy and the Environment*, 22(1): 1–35.

[iii]All the organizations listed maintain extensive websites: http://www.unglobalcompact.org/; http://www.iso.org/iso/home.htm; http://www.accountability.org/standards/index.html; http://www.oecd.org/about/.

[iv]For an overview of the development and diffusion of CSR and sustainability reporting standards, see Fifka, M. S. and Drabble, M. 2012. Focus and standardization of sustainability reporting—A comparative study of the United Kingdom and Finland. *Business Strategy and the Environment*, 21(7): 455–474; Fifka, M. S. 2013. Corporate responsibility reporting and its determinants in comparative perspective—A review of the empirical literature and a meta-analysis. *Business Strategy and the Environment*, 22(1): 1–35; Kolk, A. and Perego, P. 2010. Determinants of the adoption of sustainability assurance statements: An international investigation. *Business Strategy and the Environment*, 19(3): 182–198; Marimon, F., Alonso-Almeida, M. d. M., Rodríguez, M. d. P., and Cortez Alejandro, K. A. 2012. The worldwide diffusion of the global reporting initiative: What is the point? *Journal of Cleaner Production*, 33(2012): 132–144; Morhardt, J. E. 2010. Corporate social responsibility and sustainability reporting on the internet. *Business Strategy & the Environment*, 19(7): 436–452; Perego, P. and Kolk, A. 2012. Multinationals' accountability on sustainability: The evolution of third-party assurance of sustainability reports. *Journal of Business Ethics*, 110(2): 173–190.

[v]See Mackey, J., Friedman, M., and Rodgers, T. J. 2005. Rethinking the social responsibility of business. *Reason*, 37(5): 28–37.

[vi]Mackey, J. 2011. What conscious capitalism really is. *California Management Review*, 53(3): 83–90, pg. 83.

[vii]Mackey, J. 2011. What conscious capitalism really is. *California Management Review*, 53(3): 83–90, pg. 85.

[viii]For a thorough introduction to conscious capitalism, consult these sources: Mackey, J. 2011. What conscious capitalism really is. *California Management*

Review, 53(3): 83–90; Mackey, J., Friedman, M., and Rodgers, T. J. 2005. Rethinking the social responsibility of business. *Reason,* 37(5): 28–37; Mackey, J. and Sisodia, R. 2013. *Conscious capitalism: Liberating the heoric spirit of business.* Boston, MA: Harvard Business School Publishing; Mackey, J. and Sisodia, R. 2013. The kind of capitalist you want to be. *Harvard Business Review,* 91(1): 34–34; O'Toole, J. and Vogel, D. 2011. Two and a half cheers for conscious capitalism. *California Management Review,* 53(3): 60–76; Paumgarten, N. 2010. Food fighter. *New Yorker,* 85(43): 36–47; Sacks, D. 2009. The miracle worker. *Fast Company,* December(141): 82–89; Strong, M. 2009. *Be the solution: How entrepreneurs and conscious capitalists can solve all the world's problems.* Hoboken, NJ: John Wiley & Sons.

[ix]See Porter, M. E. and Kramer, M. R. 2006. Strategy & society: The link between competitive advantage and corporate social responsibility. *Harvard Business Review,* 84(12): 78–92.

[x]Porter, M. E. and Kramer, M. R. 2006. Strategy & society: The link between competitive advantage and corporate social responsibility. *Harvard Business Review,* 84(12): 78–92, pg. 92.

[xi]See Porter, M. E. and Kramer, M. R. 2011. Creating shared value. *Harvard Business Review,* 89(1/2): 62–77.

[xii]Porter, M. E. and Kramer, M. R. 2011. Creating shared value. *Harvard Business Review,* 89(1/2): 62–77, pg. 75.

[xiii]Acquier, A., Gond, J.-P., and Pasquero, J. 2011. Rediscovering Howard R. Bowen's legacy: The unachieved agenda and continuing relevance of *Social responsibilities of the businessman. Business & Society,* 50(4): 607–646, pg. 625.

[xiv]Hayek, F. A. 1945. The use of knowledge in society. *The American Economic Review,* 35(4): 519–530, pg. 519.

[xv]This discussion involving Hayek and CSR's ability to exploit local embedded knowledge is drawn from Beal, B. D. and Neesham, C. 2013. Systemic CSR: Insourcing the invisible hand. Tyler, TX: The University of Tyler at Texas.

[xvi]Mintzberg, H. 1983. The case for corporate social responsibility. *Journal of Business Strategy,* 4(2): 3–15, pg. 14.

[xvii]Porter, M. E. and Kramer, M. R. 2011. Creating shared value. *Harvard Business Review,* 89(1/2): 62–77, pg. 75.

References

Abbott, W. F. & Monsen, R. J. 1979. On the measurement of corporate social responsibility: Self-reported disclosures as a method of measuring corporate social involvement. *Academy of Management Journal*, 22(3): 501–515.

Acquier, A., Gond, J.-P., & Pasquero, J. 2011. Rediscovering Howard R. Bowen's legacy: The unachieved agenda and continuing relevance of *Social responsibilities of the businessman*. *Business & Society*, 50(4): 607–646.

Akerlof, G. A. 1970. The market for "lemons": Quality uncertainty and the market mechanism. *Quarterly Journal of Economics*, 84(3): 488–500.

Arthur, W. B. 1989. Competing technologies, increasing returns, and lock-in by historical events. *The Economic Journal*, 99(394): 116–131.

Aupperle, K. E., Carroll, A. B., & Hatfield, J. D. 1985. An empirical examination of the relationship between corporate social responsibility and profitability. *Academy of Management Journal*, 28(2): 446–463.

Ayres, I. & Levitt, S. D. 1998. Measuring positive externalities from unobservable victim precaution: An empirical analysis of Lojack. *Quarterly Journal of Economics*, 113(1): 43–77.

Barney, J. B. & Hesterley, W. S. 2010. *Strategic management and competitive advantage: Concepts* (3rd ed.). Upper Saddle River, NJ: Pearson Prentice Hall.

Bator, F. M. 1957. The simple analytics of welfare maximization. *American Economic Review*, 47(1): 22–59.

Bator, F. M. 1958. The anatomy of market failure. *The Quarterly Journal of Economics*, 72(3): 351–379.

Beal, B. D. 2012. Competitive markets, collective action, and the big box retailer problem. *Journal of Philosophical Economics*, 6(1): 2–29.

Beal, B. D. & Damoiseau, Y. 2007. Corporate social responsibility: Definition and the micro-to-macro problem. Tyler, TX: The University of Tyler at Texas.

Beal, B. D. & Neesham, C. 2013. Systemic CSR: Insourcing the invisible hand. Tyler, TX: The University of Tyler at Texas.

Bowen, H. R. 1953. *Social responsibilities of the businessman*. New York: Harper & Row.

Breitbarth, T., Harris, P., & Aitken, R. 2009. Corporate social responsibility in the European Union: A new trade barrier? *Journal of Public Affairs*, 9(4): 239–255.

Brown, B. & Perry, S. 1994. Removing the financial performance halo from fortune's "most admired" companies. *Academy of Management Journal*, 37(5): 1347–1359.

Brown, B. & Perry, S. 1995. Halo-removed residuals of *Fortune's* "responsibility to the community and environment": A decade of data. *Business & Society*, 34: 199–215.

Burke, L. & Logsdon, J. M. 1996. How corporate social responsibility pays off. *Long Range Planning*, 29(August): 495–502.

Carroll, A. B. 1991. The pyramid of corporate social responsibility: Toward the moral management of organizational stakeholders. *Business Horizons*, 34: 39–48.

Carroll, A. B. 1999. Corporate social responsibility: Evolution of a definitional construct. *Business and Society*, 38(3): 268–296.

Carroll, A. B. 2008. A history of corporate social responsibility: Concepts and practices. In A. Crane, A. McWilliams, D. Matten, J. Moon, & D. Siegel (Eds.), *The Oxford handbook of corporate social responsibility:* 19–46. Oxford: Oxford University Press.

Cassidy, J. 2009. *How markets fail: The logic of economic calamities.* New York: Farrar, Straus and Giroux.

Cecil, L. 2008. Corporate social responsibility reporting in the United States. *McNair Scholars Research Journal*, 1(1): Article 6.

Coleman, J. 1990. *Foundations of Social Theory.* Cambridge, MA: Harvard University Press.

Collins, D. 1996. Capitalism and sin. *Business and Society*, 35(1): 42–50.

Committee for Economic Development. 1971. *Social responsibilities of business corporations.* New York: Author.

Council on Foundations. 2012. *Increasing impact, enhancing value: A practitioner's guide to leading corporate philanthropy.*

Crane, A., McWilliams, A., Matten, D., Moon, J., & Siegel, D. 2008. The corporate social responsibility agenda. In A. Crane, A. McWilliams, D. Matten, J. Moon, & D. Siegel (Eds.), *The Oxford handbook of corporate social responsibility:* 3–15. Oxford: Oxford University Press.

Crook, C. 2005. The good company. *Economist*, 374(8410): Special Section, 3–4.

Davis, K. 1960. Can business afford to ignore social responsibilities? *California Management Review*, 2: 70–76.

Davis, K. 1967. Understanding the social responsibility puzzle: What does the businessman owe to society? *Business Horizons*, Winter: 45–50.

Davis, K. 1973. The case for and against business assumption of social responsibilities. *Academy of Management Journal*, 16(2): 312–322.

Davis, K. & Blomstrom, R. L. 1966. *Business and society: Environment and responsibility.* New York: McGraw-Hill.

Davis, K. & Blomstrom, R. L. 1971. *Business, society, and environment: Social power and social response* (2nd ed.). New York: McGraw-Hill Book Company.

Davis, K. & Blomstrom, R. L. 1975. *Business and society: Environment and responsibility* (3rd ed.). New York: McGraw-Hill.

Dawes, R. M. 1980. Social dilemmas. *Annual Review of Psychology*, 31(1): 169–193.

Fifka, M. S. 2013. Corporate responsibility reporting and its determinants in comparative perspective—A review of the empirical literature and a meta-analysis. *Business Strategy and the Environment*, 22(1): 1–35.

Fifka, M. S. & Drabble, M. 2012. Focus and standardization of sustainability reporting—A comparative study of the United Kingdom and Finland. *Business Strategy and the Environment*, 21(7): 455–474.

Fligstein, N. 2001. *The architecture of markets: An economic sociology of twenty-first century capitalist societies.* Princeton: Princeton University Press.

Frederick, W. C. 1960. The growing concern over business responsibility. *California Management Review,* 2: 54–61.

Freeman, R. E. 1984. *Strategic management: A stakeholder approach.* Boston: Pitman Publishing Inc.

Freeman, R. E., Harrison, J., Parmar, B., & de Colle, S. 2010. *Stakeholder theory: The state of the art.* Cambridge, UK: Cambridge University Press.

Freeman, R. E. & Liedtka, J. 1991. Corporate social responsibility: A critical approach. *Business Horizons,* 34(4): 92–98.

Freeman, R. E. & Velamuri, S. R. 2006. A new approach to CSR: Company stakeholder responsibility. In A. Kakabadse & M. Morsing (Eds.), *Corporate social responsibility: Reconciling aspiration with application:* 9–23. New York: Palgrave Macmillan.

Friedman, M. 1970. The social responsibility of business is to increase its profits. *New York Times Magazine,* September 13.

Fryxell, G. E. & Jia, W. 1994. The Fortune corporate 'reputation' index: Reputation for what? *Journal of Management,* 20(1): 1.

Godfrey, P. C., Merrill, C. B., & Hansen, J. M. 2009. The relationship between corporate social responsibility and shareholder value: An empirical test of the risk management hypothesis. *Strategic Management Journal,* 30(4): 425–445.

Griffin, J. J. & Mahon, J. F. 1997. The corporate social performance and corporate financial performance debate: Twenty-five years of incomparable research. *Business & Society,* 36(1): 5–31.

Hall, R. 1992. The strategic analysis of intangible resources. *Strategic Management Journal,* 13(2): 135–144.

Hayek, F. A. 1945. The use of knowledge in society. *The American Economic Review,* 35(4): 519–530.

Heckathorn, D. D. 1996. The dynamics and dilemmas of collective action. *American Sociological Review,* 61: 250–277.

Hill, C. W. L. & Jones, G. R. 2010. *Strategic management: An integrated approach* (9th ed.). Mason, OH: South-Western Cengage Learning.

Hitt, M. A., Ireland, R. D., & Hoskisson, R. E. 2009. *Strategic management concepts: Competitiveness and globalization* (8th ed.). Mason, OH: South-Western Cengage Learning.

Holme, R. & Watts, P. 2000. *Corporate social responsibility: Making good business sense:* World Business Council for Sustainable Development.

Jones, M. T. 1996. Missing the forest for the trees. *Business and Society,* 35(1): 7–41.

Karnani, A. 2010. The case against corporate social responsibility. *Wall Street Journal* (Eastern Edition), 256(45): R1–R4.

Katz, M. & Shapiro, C. 1985. Network externalities, competition and compatibility. *American Economic Review,* 75(3): 424–440.

Katz, M. L. & Shapiro, C. 1986. Technology adoption in the presence of network externalities. *Journal of Political Economy,* 94(4): 822–841.

Kolk, A. & Perego, P. 2010. Determinants of the adoption of sustainability assurance statements: An international investigation. *Business Strategy and the Environment,* 19(3): 182–198.

Kollock, P. 1998. Social dilemmas: The anatomy of cooperation. *Annual Review of Sociology,* 24: 183–214.

KPMG. 2008. International survey of corporate responsibility reporting 2008. Amsterdam: KPMG.

KPMG. 2011. International survey of corporate responsibility reporting 2011. Amsterdam: KPMG.

Kurucz, E. C., Colbert, B. A., & Wheeler, D. 2008. The business case for corporate social responsibility. In A. Crane, A. McWilliams, D. Matten, J. Moon, & D. Siegel (Eds.), *The Oxford handbook of corporate social responsibility:* 83–112. Oxford: Oxford University Press.

Kuttner, R. 1996. *Everything for sale: The virtues and limits of markets.* New York: Alfred A. Knopf.

Levitin, A. J. 2008. Priceless? The economic costs of credit card merchant restraints. *UCLA Law Review,* 55(5): 1321–1405.

Levitt, T. 1958. The dangers of social responsibility. *Harvard Business Review,* 36(5): 41–50.

Liebowitz, S. J. & Margolis, S. E. 1994. Network externality: An uncommon tragedy. *Journal of Economic Perspectives,* 8(2): 133–150.

Lindblom, C. E. 2001. *The market system: What it is, how it works, and what to make of it.* New Haven: Yale University Press.

Lockett, A., Moon, J., & Visser, W. 2006. Corporate social responsibility in management research: Focus, nature, salience and sources of influence. *Journal of Management Studies,* 43(1): 115–136.

Mackey, J. 2011. What conscious capitalism really is. *California Management Review,* 53(3): 83–90.

Mackey, J., Friedman, M., & Rodgers, T. J. 2005. Rethinking the *Social responsibility of business. Reason,* 37(5): 28–37.

Mackey, J. & Sisodia, R. 2013a. *Conscious capitalism: Liberating the heroic spirit of business.* Boston, MA: Harvard Business School Publishing.

Mackey, J. & Sisodia, R. 2013b. The kind of capitalist you want to be. *Harvard Business Review,* 91(1): 34–34.

Marens, R. 2004. Wobbling on a one-legged stool: The decline of American pluralism and the academic treatment of corporate social responsibility. *Journal of Academic Ethics,* 2(1): 63–87.

Marimon, F., Alonso-Almeida, M. d. M., Rodríguez, M. d. P., & Cortez Alejandro, K. A. 2012. The worldwide diffusion of the global reporting initiative: What is the point? *Journal of Cleaner Production,* 33(2012): 132–144.

Matten, D. & Crane, A. 2005. Corporate citizenship: Toward an extended theoretical conceptualization. *Academy of management Journal,* 30(1): 166–179.

McGuire, J. W. 1963. *Business and society.* New York: McGraw-Hill Book Company, Inc.

McWilliams, A. & Siegel, D. 2001. Corporate social responsibility: A theory of the firm perspective. *Academy of Management Review,* 26(1): 117–127.

Mintzberg, H. 1983. The case for corporate social responsibility. *Journal of Business Strategy,* 4(2): 3–15.

Moon, J., Crane, A., & Matten, D. 2005. Can corporations be citizens? Corporate citizenship as a metaphor for business participation in society. *Business Ethics Quarterly,* 15(3): 429–453.

Morhardt, J. E. 2010. Corporate social responsibility and sustainability reporting on the internet. *Business Strategy & the Environment,* 19(7): 436–452.

Murphy, P. E. 1978. An evolution: Corporate social responsiveness. *University of Michigan business review,* 6(30): 19–25.

Néron, P.-Y. & Norman, W. 2008. Citizenship, Inc. Do we really want businesses to be good corporate citizens? *Business Ethics Quarterly*, 18(1): 1–26.

O'Toole, J. & Vogel, D. 2011. Two and a half cheers for conscious capitalism. *California Management Review*, 53(3): 60–76.

Orlitzky, M. 2008. Corporate social performance and financial performance: A research synthesis. In A. Crane, A. McWilliams, D. Matten, J. Moon, & D. Siegel (Eds.), *The Oxford handbook of corporate social responsibility*: 113–134. Oxford: Oxford University Press.

Paumgarten, N. 2010. Food fighter. *New Yorker*, 85(43): 36–47.

Pepall, L., Richards, D. J., & Norman, G. 2005. *Industrial organization: Contemporary theory and practice* (3rd ed.). Mason, OH: South-Western.

Perego, P., & Kolk, A. 2012. Multinationals' accountability on sustainability: The evolution of third-party assurance of sustainability reports. *Journal of Business Ethics*, 110(2): 173–190.

Porter, M. E. & Kramer, M. R. 2006. Strategy & society: The link between competitive advantage and corporate social responsibility. *Harvard Business Review*, 84(12): 78–92.

Porter, M. E. & Kramer, M. R. 2011. Creating shared value. *Harvard Business Review*, 89(1/2): 62–77.

Pounder, B. 2011. Trends in sustainability reporting. *Strategic Finance*, 93(6): 21–23.

Rowley, T. J. & Berman, S. L. 2000. A brand new brand of corporate social performance. *Business & Society*, 39(4): 397–418.

Sacks, D. 2009. The miracle worker. *Fast Company*, December(141): 82–89.

Schelling, T. C. 1978. *Micromotives and macrobehavior*. New York: W. W. Norton & Company.

Scherer, A. G. & Palazzo, G. 2007. Toward a political conception of corporate social responsibility: Business and society seen from a Habermasian perspective. *Academy of Management Review*, 32(4): 1096–1120.

Schreck, P. 2011. Reviewing the business case for corporate social responsibility: New evidence and analysis. *Journal of Business Ethics*, 103(2): 167–188.

Shaffer, B. D. 1977. The social responsibility of business: A dissent. *Business and Society*, 17(2): 11–18.

Smith, A. 1776/1976. *An inquiry into the nature and causes of the wealth of nations*. Chicago: University of Chicago Press.

Sprinkle, G. B. & Maines, L. A. 2010. The benefits and costs of corporate social responsibility, *Business Horizons*, Vol. 53: 445–453.

Stigler, G. J. 1961. The economics of information. *Journal of Political Economy*, 69(3): 213–225.

Stiglitz, J. E. 2000. *Economics of the public sector* (3rd ed.). New York: W. W. Norton & Company.

Strong, M. 2009. *Be the solution: How entrepreneurs and conscious capitalists can solve all the world's problems*. Hoboken, NJ: John Wiley & Sons.

Swanson, D. L. 1995. Addressing a theoretical problem by reorienting the corporate social performance model. *Academy of Management Review*, 20: 43–64.

Swanson, D. L. 1999. Toward an integrative theory of business and society: A research strategy for corporate social performance. *Academy of Management Review*, 24(3): 506–521.

Tullis, P. 2011. Making the bottom line green. *Fast Company*, 154: 36–37.

Ullmann, A. A. 1985. Data in search of a theory: A critical examination of the relationships among social performance, social disclosure, and economic performance of U.S. firms. *Academy of Management Review,* 10(3): 540–557.

United Nations General Assembly. 1987. Report of the world commission on environment and development: Our common future.

Vogel, D. 2005. *The market for virtue: The potential and limits of corporate social responsiblity.* Washington, DC: Brookings Institution Press.

Vogel, D. J. 2005. Is there a market for virtue? The business case for corporate social responsibility. *California Management Review,* 47(4): 19–45.

Votaw, D. 1972. Genius becomes rare: A comment on the doctrine of social responsibility, pt. I. *California Management Review,* XV(2): 25–31.

Waddock, S. A. & Graves, S. B. 1997. The corporate social performance-financial performance link. *Strategic Management Journal,* 18(4): 303–319.

Walters, S. J. K. 1993. *Enterprise, government, and the public.* New York: McGraw-Hill.

Werther, W. B. & Chandler, D. 2011. *Strategic corporate social responsibility: Stakeholders in a global environment.* Thousand Oaks, CA: SAGE Publications, Inc.

Wheeler, D., Colbert, B., & Freeman, R. E. 2003. Focusing on value: Reconciling corporate social responsibility, sustainability and a stakeholder approach in a network world. *Journal of General Management,* 28(3): 1–28.

Wilburn, K. M. & Wilburn, R. 2011. Achieving social license to operate using stakeholder theory. *Journal of International Business Ethics,* 4(2): 3–16.

Windsor, D. 2001. Corporate citizenship: Evolution and interpretation. In J. Andriof & M. McIntosh (Eds.), *Perspectives on corporate citizenship:* 39–52. Sheffield: Greenleaf.

Wood, D. J. 1991. Corporate social performance revisited. *Academy of Management Review,* 16(4): 691–718.

Wood, D. J. 2010. Measuring corporate social performance: A review. *International Journal of Management Reviews,* 12(1): 50–84.

Wood, D. J. & Jones, R. E. 1995. Stakeholder mismatching: A theoretical problem in empirical research on corporate social performance. *International Journal of Organizational Analysis (1993–2002),* 3(3): 229.

Wood, D. J. & Logsdon, J. M. 2008. Business citizenship as metaphor and reality. *Business Ethics Quarterly,* 18(1): 51–59.

Zinkin, J. 2004. Maximising the 'licence to operate.' *Journal of Corporate Citizenship*(14): 67–80.

About the Author

Dr. Brent D. Beal is an Associate Professor of Management in the College of Business and Technology at The University of Texas at Tyler. He received his PhD in Management from the Lowry Mays College and Graduate School of Business at Texas A&M University in 2001. He has been on the faculty of the E. J. Ourso College of Business Administration at Louisiana State University and the College of Business at McNeese State University. Dr. Beal currently teaches strategic management to both undergraduates and graduate students. He conducts research in the area of corporate social responsibility and has published articles in the *Journal of Philosophical Economics*, the *Academy of Management Journal*, the *Journal of Management*, *Business Horizons*, the *Journal of Managerial Issues*, and the *Case Research Journal*.

◉SAGE research**methods**

The essential online tool for researchers from the world's leading methods publisher

Find exactly what you are looking for, from basic explanations to advanced discussion

More content and new features added this year!

"I have never really seen anything like this product before, and I think t is really valuable."
John Creswell, University of Nebraska–Lincoln

Discover **Methods Lists**— methods readings suggested by other users

Watch video interviews with leading methodologists

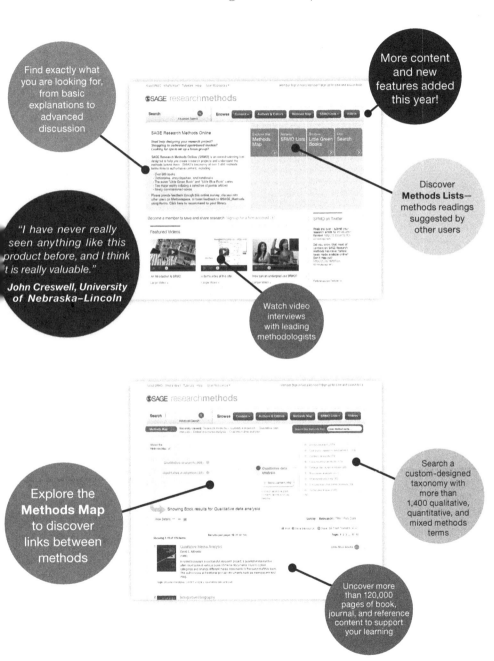

Explore the **Methods Map** to discover links between methods

Search a custom-designed taxonomy with more than 1,400 qualitative, quantitative, and mixed methods terms

Uncover more than 120,000 pages of book, journal, and reference content to support your learning

Find out more at
www.sageresearchmethods.com

Printed in the United States
By Bookmasters